Country Music Revealed

True Stories of Boozin', Cheatin', Stealin', Tax-Dodgin', and D-I-V-O-R-C-E

Randy Scott

MetroBooks

MetroBooks

AN IMPRINT OF FRIEDMAN/FAIRFAX PUBLISHERS

Library of Congress Cataloging-in-Publication Data

Scott, Randy.
Country music revealed : true stories of boozin', cheatin',
stealin', tax dodgin', and D-I-V-O-R-C-E / Randy Scott.
   p.   cm.
Includes bibliographical references and index.
ISBN 1-56799-160-2
   1. Country musicians—United States—Biography.   I. Title.
ML385.S44 1995
781.642'092'2—dc20
[B]   94-31651
                                                                         CIP
                                                                          MN

Editor: Elizabeth Viscott Sullivan
Art Director: Jeff Batzli
Designer: Susan Livingston
Photography Editors: Susan Mettler and Jennifer Crowe McMichael

Color separations by Fine Arts Repro House Co., Ltd.
Printed in China by Leefung-Asco Printers Ltd.

For bulk purchases and special sales, please contact:
Friedman/Fairfax Publishers
Attention: Sales Department
15 West 26th Street
New York, NY 10010
212/685-6610   FAX 212/685-1307

To the Visionary

Who

Invented Beer

Contents

Jerry Lee Lewis (left), country music's bad boy, once raised some hell at the gates of Graceland (above). He arrived in the middle of the night waving a pistol and inviting Elvis to come out and get his butt whipped. The King declined the offer.

Introduction

STARS DON'T *REALLY* DO THINGS MORE STUPIDLY THAN ORDINARY PEOPLE LIKE YOU AND ME—IT ONLY SEEMS THAT WAY WHEN YOU READ ABOUT THEM IN THE PAGES OF *PEOPLE* MAGAZINE, ACCOMPANIED BY THE PAPARAZZI'S UNFLATTERING MUG SHOTS.

BUT NOT ALL STARS ARE CREATED EQUAL, EITHER. WHEN A HOLLYWOOD STAR GETS CAUGHT DOING SOMETHING WRONG, IT'S USUALLY SOMETHING WORTH PUTTING ON THE FRONT PAGE OF THE NEWSPAPER. IN THE GRAND OLD DAYS, THAT MEANT FATTY ARBUCKLE RAPING AND ACCIDENTALLY KILLING A WOMAN DURING A FROLIC AT A PARTICULARLY WILD PARTY; ROBERT MITCHUM GETTING BUSTED FOR MARIJUANA BEFORE MOST PEOPLE HAD ANY IDEA WHAT IT WAS; AND FRANCES FARMER BEING TOLD SHE WAS HAVING A NERVOUS BREAKDOWN AND THRUST INTO A SANATORIUM. MORE RECENT EXAMPLES WOULD INCLUDE RIVER PHOENIX OVERDOSING OUTSIDE A LOS ANGELES NIGHTCLUB, KIM BASINGER LOSING A $9 MILLION LAWSUIT FOR RENEGING ON A FILM COMMITMENT, AND SHARON STONE STEALING SOMEONE'S HUSBAND.

THINGS TEND TO HAPPEN A BIT DIFFERENTLY IN THE WORLD OF ROCK MUSIC, HOWEVER. THE MISDEEDS HERE TEND TO BE MORE OUTRÉ, MORE RIDICULOUS. WHETHER IT'S JIM MORRISON GETTING ARRESTED FOR EXPOSING HIMSELF ONSTAGE DURING A PERFORMANCE, BRIAN JONES FLOATING FACEDOWN IN HIS SWIMMING POOL AFTER A DRUG OVERDOSE, OR MICHAEL JACKSON BEING SUED FOR $100 MILLION BY THE FAMILY OF A YOUNG OVERNIGHT CAMPER, IT'S CLEAR THAT ROCK STARS DON'T ALWAYS POSSESS COMMON SENSE.

WHICH BRINGS US TO THE WORLD OF COUNTRY MUSIC, WHERE "WHITE LIGHTNIN'S STILL THE GREATEST THRILL OF ALL," AS MERLE HAGGARD SANG IN ONE OF HIS MOST FAMOUS SONGS. (YOU KNOW MERLE—HE'S THE NO-NONSENSE OUTLAW WHO EARNED HIS STINT IN THE JOINT BY TRYING TO ROB A BAR ONE CHRISTMAS EVE; HE BROKE IN THROUGH THE BACK DOOR WHILE THE PLACE WAS FILLED WITH CUSTOMERS IN THE MIDST OF THEIR REVELRY.) BUT WHITE LIGHTNING WOULD SOON BE SUPPLANTED BY—AND OFTEN MIXED WITH—WHITE POWDER, EVEN IN THE HALLOWED HALLS OF NASHVILLE. IN NO TIME AT ALL, THE KINGS AND QUEENS OF COUNTRY MUSIC WOULD BE OUTDOING THEIR MORE DAZZLING BIG-

SCREEN AND ROCK 'N' ROLL BRETHREN WITH SHENANIGANS SO TACKY, SO SILLY, SO *DUMB* THAT THE ANNUAL AWARDS FOR FOOLISH BEHAVIOR AND ABSURD ACCIDENTS MIGHT AS WELL BE HANDED OUT ON THE STAGE OF THE GRAND OLE OPRY.

SURE, JIM MORRISON SHOULD HAVE BEEN ASHAMED OF HIMSELF FOR WHIPPING IT OUT IN FRONT OF HIS FLORIDA AUDIENCE. BUT AT LEAST HE NEVER SERENADED THE CROWD IN THE VOICE OF DONALD DUCK, AS COUNTRY LEGEND GEORGE "NO SHOW" JONES ONCE DID, JUST BEFORE THEY HAULED HIM OFF TO AN ASYLUM. (YOU KNOW GEORGE—HE ONCE RODE HIS POWER LAWN MOWER TEN MILES [16KM] OR MORE TO GET A DRINK WHEN HE FOUND HIS PALATIAL ESTATE WAS DRY.)

SURE, MICHAEL JACKSON DEMONSTRATED POOR JUDGMENT IN ALLOWING THE APPEARANCE (AT LEAST) OF WRONGDOING WITH HIS LITTLE PLAYMATE. BUT AT LEAST HE DIDN'T MARRY A THIRTEEN-YEAR-OLD COUSIN BEFORE HIS DIVORCE FROM HIS FIRST WIFE WAS EVEN FINALIZED AND HAUL THE KID OFF TO ENGLAND TO MEET THE QUEEN, AS JERRY LEE LEWIS DID BACK IN 1957. (YOU KNOW JERRY LEE—THE GUY WHO ARRIVED AT THE GATES OF GRACELAND IN THE MIDDLE OF THE NIGHT WAVING A PISTOL AND INVITING ELVIS TO C'MON OUTSIDE TO GET HIS BUTT WHIPPED. ELVIS, DEEP INTO A PEANUT BUTTER 'N' BACON SANDWICH, APPARENTLY DECLINED.) BUT POOR JUDGMENT DOESN'T HARM THE CAREER OF A C&W STAR THE WAY IT DOES POLITICIANS, MOVIE STARS, AND THOSE OF US IN OTHER WALKS OF LIFE. ODDLY ENOUGH, IT SOMETIMES SEEMS TO HELP. WHEN GLEN CAMPBELL STOLE AWAY THE WIFE OF GOOD FRIEND MAC DAVIS MANY YEARS AGO, ALL THAT HAPPENED WAS THAT HE WON A GRAMMY AND SEVERAL OTHER AWARDS AND SAW HIS RECORD SALES HIT AN ALL-TIME HIGH. COMPARE THAT TO THE BLACKLISTING INGRID BERGMAN RECEIVED WHEN SHE LEFT HER DOCTOR HUSBAND TO TAKE UP WITH ITALIAN DIRECTOR ROBERTO ROSSELLINI. (GRANTED, SHE NEVER CUT A GREAT TUNE LIKE "RHINESTONE COWBOY.")

THERE'S SOMETHING ALMOST SWEET ABOUT THE WAY COUNTRY MUSIC STARS SCREW UP, COMPARED TO THE FOIBLES OF OTHER KINDS OF ENTERTAINERS. ROCK STARS JIMI HENDRIX, JANIS JOPLIN, AND KEITH MOON ALL MET UGLY ENDS, EITHER OVERDOSING ON HEROIN OR ASPHYXIATING ON THEIR VOMIT WHILE PASSED OUT COLD—BUT NEAR-OVERDOSE VICTIM HANK WILLIAMS, JR., SURVIVED HIS BRUSH WITH CHEMICAL DEATH ONLY TO FALL DOWN A MOUNTAIN AND NEARLY GET KILLED ALL OVER AGAIN. (CAN YOU PICTURE JIMI HENDRIX FALLING DOWN A MOUNTAIN? IT'S JUST TOO *HEALTHY* A CONCEPT.) THE

Introduction

WHO WERE FAMOUS FOR DESTROYING THEIR HOTEL ROOMS, AND THE ROLLING STONES FOR THEIR DE-PRAVED SEXUAL APPETITES, BUT JOHNNY CASH'S WORST MISTAKE WAS ACCIDENTALLY SETTING A NA-TIONAL PARK ON FIRE WHEN HE FLIPPED A CIGARETTE BUTT OUT HIS CAR WINDOW. AND POOR WILLIE NELSON GOT NAILED BY THE INTERNAL REVENUE SERVICE FOR UNDERPAYING HIS TAXES WHEN ALL HE HAD TO DO WAS ASK MICK AND KEITH TO FIND HIM A VILLA NEXT DOOR TO THEM IN THE SOUTH OF FRANCE TO KEEP ANYONE FROM EVER BOTHERING HIM ABOUT ANYTHING SO TACKY IN THE FIRST PLACE. (AND, BY GOD, THAT'S JUST WHAT THE KILLER, JERRY LEE LEWIS HIMSELF, ENDED UP DOING A FEW YEARS BACK, ONLY *HIS* TICKET WAS PUNCHED FOR IRELAND.)

BUT THAT KIND OF THINKING DEMANDS COMMON SENSE, AND IF THERE'S ONE THING IN SHORT SUP-PLY IN NASHVILLE, IT WOULD SEEM TO BE THAT. HOW ELSE CAN YOU EXPLAIN JOHNNY PAYCHECK EARN-ING HIMSELF A COUPLE OF YEARS IN PRISON FOR SHOOTING A GUY IN A BAR WHILE ARGUING OVER TURTLE MEAT? EVEN SEAN PENN NEVER GOT INTO A FIGHT OVER ANYTHING *THAT* DUMB.

WHAT IT ALL COMES DOWN TO IS THE DIFFERENCE BETWEEN JIM MORRISON EXPOSING HIMSELF ONSTAGE AND LORETTA LYNN FAINT-ING ONSTAGE, BETWEEN MADONNA MAKING A FOOL OF HERSELF ON *THE LATE SHOW WITH DAVID LETTERMAN* WITH HER FOUL MOUTH AND DOLLY PARTON LEADING THE WAY IN JOKING ABOUT HERSELF AND HER VICTORIA'S SECRET WARDROBE. (AND WHERE WOULD *YOU* RATHER SPEND A DAY, WITH OR WITHOUT THE KIDS: DOLLYWOOD OR MADONNAWOOD? I THOUGHT SO.)

SO LET US NOW SALUTE THE GREATS OF COUNTRY MUSIC, WHO IN THEIR MOMENTS OF WEAKNESS HAVE DONE THE GOL-DANGEST THINGS, MORE OFTEN TO THEM-SELVES THAN TO OTHERS—THE KINDS OF THINGS THAT, WHEN YOU READ ABOUT THEM, MAKE YOU SHAKE YOUR HEAD AND MUTTER IN RELUCTANT ADMIRATION, "DAMN— *THAT'S* COUNTRY!"

HANK
WILLIAMS,
SR.

MERLE
HAGGARD

JERRY LEE
LEWIS

HANK
WILLIAMS, JR.
(WITH
HANK III)

Born to Raise Hell

Hank Williams, Sr.

I'm So Lonesome
I Could Die

The older he got, the more closely he assumed the aspect of a tragic buffoon—a tall, balding man of no particular learning who possessed a big talent housed in a frail body and a frailer psyche, which in the end proved to be the end of him. And yet Hiriam (as "Hiram" was

misspelled on his birth certificate) Williams still bestrides the landscape of country music like a giant, more than forty years after his excesses snuffed out his flame forever. Or, as Hank once darkly warned an audience, "Y'all don't worry, 'cause it ain't gonna be all right nohow."

Born in 1923 in Mount Olive, Alabama, with spina bifida, a disease that permanently weakened his constitution, he was raised by his mother, Lilly, from the age of seven after his father, Lonnie, succumbed to a number of old World War I injuries and had to move to a Veteran's Administration hospital in Alexandria, Louisiana. With no money coming in, Lilly moved the family to Georgiana, Alabama, and sent Hank into the streets to sell peanuts, shine shoes, peddle seed packets—anything that might earn a coin or two. Lilly soon was running a boardinghouse and doing better financially, but young Hank liked being on the street. When he was twelve, he formed a bond with one Rufus Payne, a black street singer who called himself Tee-Tot and taught his willing admirer how to sing the blues, pick a guitar, and drink beer—not necessarily in that order.

Hank learned at Tee-Tot's knee for two years, missing much of his formal schooling in the process. But he bade his mentor farewell when Lilly moved the family to the more upscale burg of Montgomery, affording Hank the opportunity to cut classes in a better school. He began entering—and winning—singing contests, and formed his first band, the Drifting Cowboys, when he was just fifteen; with that, he became a hillbilly singer for real, just as he'd aspired to be. But Lilly still expected him to finish school, so after playing most nights with the band in bars and clubs, he'd show up for class—still half-drunk and completely exhausted. By 1942, he was nineteen years old and had only made it as far as the ninth grade. At that point, he decided enough was enough, and dropped out of school to perform full-time. By now he was also drinking full-time.

It was while performing that year that his eye wandered to an attractive woman in the audience. The woman turned out to be a drugstore clerk named Audrey Mae Sheppard Guy—and she was married. But not for long; she divorced her GI husband while he was fighting overseas and invited Hank to move in with her. Two years later, in December 1944, Hank and Audrey were married at a gas station in Andalusia, Alabama. Hank's life would never be the same. Audrey was ambitious, and Hank couldn't think of any good reasons not to go along with her master plan for his career, so he did. Whatever her faults—and they were legion—Audrey's fervent determination improved Hank's attendance record for his performances, the spottiness of which would continue to plague him until his dying day.

More important, it was Audrey who dragged Hank into the Acuff-Rose offices in Nashville, landing him his first songwriting contract. Fred Rose also decided to send Hank on tour in order to give his songs wider exposure. The strategy worked: early in 1947, Hank was given a recording contract with the tiny Sterling Records label. He had some regional hits and showed enough promise for MGM to tender him a contract. Audrey jumped at the chance, and Hank had his first national hit, the infectious "Move It on Over," which in turn gave Fred Rose ammunition to convince the popular radio showcase *Louisiana Hayride* to sign Hank as a regular. In May 1948 Hank and Audrey moved to Shreveport. With the help of *Hayride*, hit after hit followed—"Hey, Good Lookin'," "I'm So Lonesome I Could Die," and the enormous smash "Lovesick

Blues." Hank's battle with the bottle was doomed to fail, but Audrey helped keep his thirst in check—although at one point she actually filed for divorce (it seems that Hank had been getting too frisky with his gun collection).

In May 1949, Randall Hank Williams (Hank, Jr.) was born to Audrey and Hank, and all was joy at the Williams household. A month later, Hank made his debut on the *Grand Ole Opry* show, his last hurdle to superstardom. As Minnie Pearl, who performed alongside Hank at the Opry, recalled, "He had a real animal magnetism; he just destroyed the women in the audience." That wasn't all he did to those women; he invited some of the younger ones to spend the night with him, a hobby that of course came to Audrey's attention soon enough. She'd angrily confront Hank when he dragged

Opposite: The one, the only, the dear-departed Hank Williams. If only his life had been as happy as he looks here. Above: Audrey and Hank with their children, Lucretia (Audrey's daughter from her first marriage) and Hank, Jr., in a rare moment of domestic bliss.

himself home in the wee hours, and he'd absorb her harangue until he either passed out cold or clipped her on the jaw.

But Audrey turned the other cheek as much as she was able to, because Hank was now a money-making machine. "Why Don't You Love Me (Like You Used to Do)?" "You're Gonna Change," and "Long Gone Lonesome Blues" all charted high in 1949 and 1950, and in 1951 Hank had seven Top Ten hits, which at the time must have been some sort of record.

As his star rose higher, Hank went back to drinking in earnest, which he augmented with handfuls of Benzedrine to pick himself up enough to perform. Despite the pills, he began missing more and more dates, and even when he made one on time, he'd forget half the lyrics to his songs. Finally, he did the un-

thinkable: he began showing up drunk at his dates at the Opry. "The Opry people gave him plenty of chances," Faron Young recalled. "They'd run him off for a while and he'd come back and be drunk all over again." Sometimes he'd disappear for weeks at a time.

Realizing he was in trouble, Hank agreed to check himself in to Vanderbilt Hospital to dry out. He did, for about fifteen minutes; with the help of his mother, he checked himself out just as quickly. Before she had driven him a mile (1.6km) from the hospital, he was inaugurating another three-week toot.

Hank's addictions were increased by his ever-worsening back pain, a chronic condition exacerbated by a horseback-riding injury that began to require its own megadoses of painkillers. He had a spinal fusion in the autumn of 1951 to repair the ruptured discs, but

The Opry in all its Grand Ole glory. Hank ruled here until an ocean of booze, painkillers, amphetamines, and assorted other pharmaceuticals washed away his career and, finally, his life.

the pain didn't subside. His nerves were shot, and so were the walls and television sets of his hotel rooms, which he regularly used for target practice. (He even aimed and fired at a maid once, who wisely knocked him out with a table lamp.)

Audrey's response to all of this craziness was to spend Hank's money as fast as he could make it—and he made a lot—and to find herself some gentlemen friends of her own. Hank's "Your Cheatin' Heart" and "Cold, Cold Heart" may have been recriminating Audrey, although she wasn't doing anything he hadn't done a hundred times. But after Hank opened fire on Audrey and two of her friends at a New Year's Eve party, she decided she'd had enough and filed for divorce in January 1952. Audrey got the divorce, and the house, the Caddy, Hank, Jr., Lucretia, $1,000 a month

in alimony, and half of all Hank's future royalties, too. The Opry trumped the divorce by quietly refusing to allow him to perform after August 1952. Hank was practically run out of Nashville on a rail.

Back in Alabama with Lilly, he landed a gig immediately on the *Louisiana Hayride* show, but those mounting losses still stung. He applied balm in the form of nineteen-year-old Billie Jean Jones Eshmiller, a drop-dead gorgeous Nashville divorcée he had met backstage at one of his final Opry appearances. The couple were married (over Lilly's objections) on October 18, 1952—not once, not twice, but *three* times, the extra ceremonies performed before paying customers ($1.50 and 75¢ per ticket) at the Municipal Auditorium in New Orleans. The total take provided a rather hefty dowry of $30,000 for a Cuba honeymoon—or would have, if Hank hadn't been so drunk that the vacation had to be canceled.

Nonetheless, he was still country's best-selling star—"Jambalaya" was his latest number-one hit, and "Honky Tonk Blues" had also reached the top—but at home he couldn't even go to the bathroom by himself. Young Billie Jean didn't know how to care for her drug-addicted, near-invalid husband, so on December 11, 1952, she and her brother committed him to Shreveport's North Louisiana Sanitarium to help him get straight—but the treatment didn't take. Then came the news that a previous flame, Bobbie Webb Jett, had given birth to his daughter, Cathy (see page 33). He promised to pay Jett child support, which probably did not improve the climate much at home.

Sicker and weaker than ever, Hank hired a "doctor," a quack named Toby Marshall, for $300 a week to administer chloral hydrate, possibly in lieu of alcohol, which knocked him out as soon as he'd take a dose. And Hank being Hank, he didn't stop drinking anyway, which meant that his system was constantly flooded with unmonitored dosages of painkillers, chloral hydrate, and Benzedrine, which he washed down with beer and vodka. It was enough to kill a horse—and more than enough to kill Hank.

On New Year's Eve, 1952, his plane flight canceled because of bad weather, Hank was being driven by chauffeur Charles Carr to Canton, Ohio, where he was scheduled to perform the evening of January 1. En route, Hank passed out in the backseat of his baby blue Cadillac, and an alarmed Carr stopped at a hotel in Knoxville, where he asked for a doctor to be called. A Dr. P.H. Cardwell arrived with one hypodermic needle full of morphine and another of B-12, both of which he injected into the semiconscious Hank. (Carr, who is still alive as of this writing, contends that both injections were vitamins.)

Carr ate dinner at the hotel, then had two porters carry the sleeping Hank—who may have expired already—back to the car. The journey to Canton was resumed, although Carr was stopped for reckless driving by Swann Kitts of the Tennessee Highway Patrol. The sight of the comatose Williams aroused Kitts' suspicions, but Carr reassured him that the singer had merely passed out per usual, so the officer let them go after Carr paid a $25 fine. (Much later Kitts filed a report that stated: "I think Williams was dead when he was dressed and carried out of the [Knoxville] hotel." But the world didn't learn of that theory until almost thirty years later.)

When Carr pulled into a gas station in Oak Hill, West Virginia, early on New Year's morning, he noticed that Hank was stiff as a board and rushed the body to the Oak Hill Hospital, where Hank Williams was pronounced dead on arrival.

Lilly was quickly called to the scene, where she made certain that Hank's death certificate read "heart failure." (Many suspect she had the autopsy report sanitized to preserve his dignity; a fair question might be, "What dignity?") A crowd of more than twenty thousand assembled for the funeral (arranged by Audrey and Lilly without so much as consulting Billie Jean) in Montgomery a few days later. Roy Acuff, Red Foley, and Ernest Tubb were among the stars who sang tributes, and the service was broadcast by two radio stations. Both Audrey and Billie Jean arrived in black, but Lilly stood only with Audrey, a foreshadowing of events to come, for Audrey and Lilly were about to embark on a decades-long struggle in the courts with Billie Jean for control of Hank's rich musical legacy, a legacy that paid immediate dividends

George Hamilton, Jr., wasn't very convincing as a country boy—that cocoa-butter tan hardly resembled Hank's hard-earned pallor!—but he faked his way through the eleven tunes in Your Cheatin' Heart, *the film version of Hank's life, thanks to fifteen-year-old Hank, Jr.'s dubbing.*

I'LL NEVER GET OUT OF THIS WORLD ALIVE

HANK WILLIAMS AND FRED ROSE

Recorded by HANK WILLIAMS for MGM Records

MILENE MUSIC
2510 FRANKLIN ROAD
NASHVILLE 4, TENNESSEE

SOLE SELLING AGENTS
ACUFF-ROSE PUBLICATIONS
2510 FRANKLIN ROAD, NASHVILLE 4, TENN.

Hank wrote "I'll Never Get Out of This World Alive," and he was right about that. But he might have waited another forty years or so, for the sake of those he left behind.

when two of Hank's newly recorded songs, "Kaw-Liga" and "Your Cheatin' Heart," were released soon after his death and became smash hits.

Some of the legal battles that surround Hank's work are still being waged; collectively, they are worthy of an entire book. There may never be enough space to weigh the contributions Hank made in elevating country music into a truly national (and, today, international) industry, one that earns billions where once nickels and dimes were harvested. The trauma visited upon Hank, Jr., who was three when Hank died, is discussed later in this chapter, but he has remarked many times of the belated appreciation of his father, "They hated Daddy in Nashville." Yet is it just hypocrisy that inspired June Carter's comment about

his passing: "We loved him, we lost him, and we still miss him"? Perhaps, but more likely the sentiment is sincere.

The 1964 MGM movie about Hank's life, *Your Cheatin' Heart*, was made with Audrey's approval and Hank, Jr.'s voice, but it's hard to see the demons that haunted Hank reflected on the tanned visage of George Hamilton, Jr. A more enduring memorial to Hank was, appropriately, penned by the great man himself the year before he died. Chillingly, its prescient title was "I'll Never Get Out of This World Alive." But then, none of us do.

Jerry Lee Lewis

MIDDLE AGE CRAZY

The enigma known as Jerry Lee Lewis, the wild talent behind such rock 'n' roll classics of the fifties as "Whole Lotta Shakin' Goin' On" and "Great Balls of Fire," had to rebound from a career-crushing international scandal before he was finally able to re-cast himself as a C&W chart-topper. He's a maker of great music, to be sure, and a performer with few peers—but also a man prone to frightening outbursts of unprovoked violence. His sobriquet, "The Killer," refers to what he does to a piano in the throes of a performance, but it has taken on a more sinister connotation over the years. Entire books have been written that try to plumb his depths, most notably Nick Tosches' brilliant *Hellfire* and Charles White's oral history. Both are highly recommended, but for those who haven't the time to absorb their lessons, a shortcut into Jerry Lee's twisted psyche is provided by some of his typically deft bons mots:

ON THE DEATH OF ELVIS:

"I WAS GLAD. JUST ANOTHER ONE OUT OF THE WAY.... HE WAS A WEAKLING, MAN."

Jerry Lee performing in 1983.

ON THE FREQUENT LEGAL CHARGES FROM WIVES AND OTHERS CHARGING HIM WITH ABUSIVE BEHAVIOR AND ASSAULT:

> "I NEVER HIT ANYBODY—
> UNLESS I WANT TO."

ON THE SUDDEN SUPERSTARDOM OF WAYLON JENNINGS AND WILLIE NELSON:

> "I DON'T LIKE THAT HILLBILLY SHIT."

ON THE OUTRAGED RESPONSE OF THE PRESS TO HIS DECEMBER 1957 MARRIAGE TO HIS THIRTEEN-YEAR-OLD SECOND COUSIN, MYRA GALE BROWN:

> "I WANTED TO GET MARRIED; I GOT
> MARRIED. THEY DON'T LIKE IT,
> THEY CAN KISS MY BUTT."

TO FORMER WIFE MYRA GALE:

> "IF YOU EVER LEAVE ME AGAIN, I'LL
> THROW ACID IN YOUR FACE."

ON WHETHER HIS SIX MARRIAGES HAVE TAUGHT HIM ANYTHING ABOUT WOMEN:

> "YEAH—(**CENSORED**)."

So maybe you *wouldn't* want to spend a week in a cabin with the guy—especially if you knew that he shot Butch Owens, a member of his band, in the chest at point-blank range with a .357 Magnum back in 1975. "Look down the barrel of this," Jerry Lee told the bewildered bass player, before pulling the trigger. (That little stunt cost The Killer a cool $125,000 in damages awarded by a jury—cheap at twice the price, considering what the penalty would have been if Owens had died.)

Then there was the mysterious death of ex-wife number four, Jaren, who was found drowned at the bottom of her swimming pool in 1982. A tragic accident, no doubt—but not long before her demise, she had sworn in a document submitted to the court overseeing her divorce proceedings that Jerry Lee told her to desist from requesting child support payments because "if you don't get off my back and leave me alone, you will end up in the bottom of the lake at the farm with chains around you."

By then Jerry Lee was already seeing twenty-four-year-old Shawn Michelle Stephens, whom he married almost a year to the day after Jaren's body was fished out of that Memphis pool. Less than three months later, on August 24, 1983, Shawn's bloody, beaten corpse was found lying in the bed of the couple's Mississippi home just one day after the young bride phoned her mother to confide that the marriage was over. As reported in *Rolling Stone*, the blood-splattered crime scene, the deep scratches on the back of Jerry Lee's hand, and the blood on his clothes somehow led the coroner to conclude that Shawn had killed herself by overdosing on methadone—determined after an autopsy was conducted by a doctor who was hired and paid by Jerry Lee Lewis. (Where's Perry Mason when you need him?)

Eight months later Jerry Lee married a twenty-two-year-old wanna-be singer, Kerrie Lynn McCarver.

Why is this man not laughing? A dour Jerry Lee stands next to new bride Shawn Michelle Stephens on their wedding day. If only Shawn had looked deeply into Jerry's psycho eyes, she might have guessed what was in store for her.

To no one's surprise, she soon filed for divorce on the grounds of abusive treatment after Jerry Lee punched her in the nose and "cursed, threatened, and struck her on occasions too numerous to mention." (No, no—mention them!) But after she bore him a boy—Jerry Lee Lewis III—in 1987, the couple reconciled. "I never hit a woman in my life," Jerry Lee told talk-show host Geraldo Rivera with a straight face while guesting on his program. (It's amazing that a lightning bolt didn't come down from the sky and toast him right on national television.)

Born in Ferriday, Louisiana, on September 29, 1935, Jerry Lee was a typical wild kid who used to play the piano at the Fundamentalist Assembly of God Church and cut classes with his no-account cousins, Jimmy Lee Swaggart and Mickey Gilley. But unlike them and most other people in the world, he grew up to be an atypically wild adult. Fortunately for him, he had a large talent and began cutting records for Sam Phillips at Sun Records in 1956, just after Phillips sold Elvis Presley's past and future rights to RCA for $40,000. Jerry Lee's first tunes enjoyed some regional popularity, and he also labored as a session pianist on other artists' records.

He burst onto the national music scene in the summer of 1957 with "Whole Lotta Shakin' Goin' On." After he performed the song twice on *The Steve Allen Show*, it began selling ten thousand copies a day, each and every day, for months on end. He was riding high on the pop, country, and R&B charts, and it began to seem possible that he might even overtake Elvis; after all, there was no Colonel Parker pulling Jerry Lee's strings, trying to rein in the raw sexual magnetism that was his first claim to fame. The frenzy Jerry Lee created when he sang and beat the living hell out of his piano, long blond locks flying every which way, was enough to make those bobby-soxers forget about that cat from Memphis—who in December 1957 was in-

*"**Come** along, honey, it's your lover-boy, me, that's a-knockin'"—that's how Jerry Lee kicked off the opening stanza of the great theme song to* High School Confidential. *The song would be his last Top-Five hit for many years to come as a result of his scandalous marriage to his thirteen-year-old second cousin, Myra Gale Brown.*

formed by the federal government that he was about to be shipped overseas to Germany for an army hitch, leaving his throne vacant for the next two years.

Since Jerry Lee was the kind of tough guy who would never record those syrupy ballads that Elvis so often crooned—schmaltz like "Love Me Tender" and "Loving You"—even guys could be his fans without looking too soft. If "Great Balls of Fire," his follow-up smash, wasn't an anthem for tumescent high school studs, what was?

Jerry Lee was everywhere. He was costarring with Fats Domino in *Jamboree*, a rock movie. He was about to appear in *High School Confidential*, a film that opens with Jerry Lee pounding out the title track from

the back of a moving flatbed truck. He was back on *The Steve Allen Show*, and every other television variety showcase as well. He headlined with Chuck Berry in Alan Freed's *Big Beat* show, burning his piano to the ground at the Brooklyn Paramount because Chuck had been selected over him to close the show; the crowd loved it. Yes, the possibilities were boundless.

But then Jerry Lee shot himself in the foot—no, make that *both* feet. On December 12, 1957, he married his second cousin, Myra Gale Brown, the daughter of J.W. Brown, the bass player in his band. Which would have been fine, except the lady was a thirteen-year-old, eighth-grade dropout. In the Mississippi Delta where Jerry Lee grew up, marrying a thirteen-year-old

The honeymooners. The combined *ages of Jerry Lee and Myra Gale equaled thirty-five when the two married in December 1957. Maybe things would have been better had they waited until Myra had finished the eighth grade—or if she hadn't met the press in that hat.*

two weeks earlier. That was all shocking enough, but then a Memphis reporter picked up the story, did some digging, and found that Myra's birth certificate listed her as being born on July 11, 1944, making her only thirteen. The London tabloids went berserk, the audiences at his London performances booed when they bothered to show up at all, and the rest of the tour was canceled.

Back in the United States, Jerry Lee found that the standards of rural Louisiana were not enough to sway the national press, which gleefully reported that he had been expelled from England as an undesirable alien. His dates in the States dried up as suddenly as a creek does in the heat of July. Just as quickly as it had ignited, his once-blazing popularity had been reduced to a few embers in a pile of cold ashes. He couldn't get airplay from rock stations, and when he covered Hank Williams' "Cold, Cold Heart" in 1959, the C&W stations barely acknowledged it.

wasn't so weird, but elsewhere it was considered robbing the cradle—which was why the couple filled in Myra's age as twenty on the marriage certificate. There was one other little problem: Jerry Lee wasn't officially divorced yet from his second wife, Jane Mitcham Lewis. But no one was really aware of that fact for the time being, since the marriage was being kept a secret.

The story broke in May 1958, as Jerry Lee embarked on his thirty-seven-day, thirty-show British tour. As he was traveling with Myra, Jerry 'fessed up to the British press—sort of—and told about their marriage, giving her age as fifteen. He also fudged the dates on his divorce from Jane, which had been finalized about

On the eve of his first return to England, in April 1962, tragedy struck: his three-year-old son, Steve Allen—named for the man who had given Jerry Lee his big break—was found drowned in the family pool. After the funeral, Jerry Lee did the tour, which was such a great success that he was invited back for another visit. Ironically, he was now a big star overseas, playing to packed houses in England, Germany, and France; it was his homeland that continued to ignore him. He was making a living, but there was no glory. He made records, but nobody ever heard or bought them. He was yesterday's news. (He also narrowly escaped a jail term in 1965 when his band was arrested after police found hundreds of pills—amphetamines, mostly—behind the seat of Jerry Lee's Cadillac. Since band members were in the car and he wasn't, they took the fall. But the pills were his, as were any number of empty whiskey bottles.)

Jerry Lee's ten years in the wilderness ended when, as a last-ditch effort, Eddie Kilroy convinced him (and, not incidentally, Smash Records) to record an album of new country music in Nashville in January 1968. One of the songs from that session, "Another Place, Another Time," saved Jerry Lee's career, as it registered on both the C&W and pop charts. Even bigger hits followed—"What's Made Milwaukee Famous (Has Made a Loser Out of Me)," "She Still Comes Around (To Love What's Left of Me)," and "She Even Woke Me up to Say Goodbye." There wasn't an ounce of rock 'n' roll in any of the songs, but they announced as surely as anything could that The Killer was back.

Fame, sweet fame, was within his grasp again, but Jerry Lee was showing signs of being wound a few turns too tight. When Myra Gale filed for divorce in November 1970 (wisely, while he was touring Australia), Jerry Lee swore off alcohol and even refused to play in venues (like nightclubs) where liquor was served, but to no avail: Myra was gone. She left him the house, but took their seven-year-old daughter, a hunk of cash, and their Lincoln Continentals. Then in a nice bit of poetic justice, she married the private detective who turned up the goods on Jerry Lee's philandering, making the decree a foregone conclusion. A few months later, Jerry Lee married Jaren Elizabeth Gunn Pate, a Memphis divorcée. Two weeks later, Jerry Lee and Jaren separated. Then they reconciled. Then they had a baby.

All the while, the hits kept coming, such as "Chantilly Lace" and "Would You Take Another Chance on Me?" In 1973, he made his triumphal debut at the Opry, but that was also the year that his other son by Myra, Jerry Lee, Jr.—a chronic drug abuser and a drummer in the band—was killed when his Jeep overturned. And then there was the time in 1975 that Jerry Lee shot Butch Owens...the night in 1976 when he drove up to the gates of Graceland at 4 A.M. brandishing a gun and demanding to see Elvis, who understandably called the Memphis cops...the visits to the Memphis Mental Health Institute...the 1979 arrest for possession of narcotics...the 1981 command performance at Memphis Methodist Hospital, where two emergency operations on his perforated stomach managed (just barely) to save his life...the mysterious deaths of ex-wife Jaren and then–current wife Shawn...the 1984 indictment for tax evasion (he didn't have a hit song called "Middle Age Crazy" for

They call him "The Killer"—and you can see why. Jerry Lee's scary visage speaks volumes about what he's seen—and what he's done—in decades of hard, hard living.

nothing)…all topped off by his self-imposed exile to Ireland to avoid having all his performance fees attached by the Internal Revenue Service.

Quite a track record when you put it all together—and a long, long way from playing the piano during church services. One has to imagine what Jerry Lee thought of Myra's book about him, *Great Balls of Fire*, not to mention its 1989 movie version. (Originally the film was to star screw-loose actor Mickey Rourke—a match made in heaven— but in the end Dennis Quaid starred as The Killer, with Winona Ryder as Myra. Quaid hardly suggested being tormented by cracker demons, although his lip-synching to Jerry Lee's voice is beyond reproach.) Now, Jerry Lee is back from Ireland, ready to work off his debt to the government. But will his story have a happy ending? Lest we forget, Jerry Lee once remarked to an unfortunate soul, "You scared of me? You should be. Why do you think they call me 'The Killer'?"

Merle Haggard

PROUD TO BE AN OKIE FROM SAN QUENTIN

George Jones may have been more of a screwup, and Johnny Paycheck was meaner, but Merle Haggard took a backseat to no one as country music's premier badass. When he was a kid he was a full-fledged juvenile delinquent, and when he grew up he was an adult delinquent. But through it all—and there was a lot of trouble to wade through—Merle's music never suffered. In fact, it was the better for all the mayhem.

Born in 1937 in Bakersfield, California, where the Depression still maintained a stranglehold, Merle was raised by parents who had migrated there, like the Okies in John Steinbeck's *The Grapes of Wrath*, in 1934. As a kid, Merle seemed born for trouble, and he found it early and often. When his father, a fiddle player, died of a brain tumor when Merle was just nine, his mother—a Church of Christ devotee—watched helplessly as her son spun out of control. At fourteen, Merle was put in the Fred C. Nelles School for Boys in Whittier, California, from which he escaped, as he did from the Preston School of Industry in Stockton a year later. By the time he was eighteen, he had been arrested for car theft (earning a nine-month jail term) and passing bad checks. In between arrests, he picked

Pop Quiz

Those old-timers had one thing over today's young stars— better nicknames! Match the handle with the performer:

1. "The Possum"
2. "The Singing Sheriff"
3. "The Singing Fisherman"
4. "The Tennessee Plowboy"
5. "The Singing Ranger"
6. "King of the Cowboys"
7. "The Drifting Cowboy"
8. "Mr. Guitar"
9. "The Silver Fox"
10. "The Park Avenue Hillbilly"

A. Hank Williams
B. Del Wood
C. Roy Rogers
D. George Jones
E. Johnny Horton
F. Chet Atkins
G. Eddy Arnold
H. Hank Snow
I. Faron Young
J. Charlie Rich

Answers: 1-D, 2-I, 3-E, 4-G, 5-H, 6-C, 7-A, 8-F, 9-J, 10-B

crops for wages and hoboed across the Southwest. "Being behind bars was almost beginning to be a way of life," he once reflected. "I didn't like it, but I didn't like life on the outside, either."

At this point in his life, Merle didn't have to worry much about life on the outside. On Christmas Eve in 1957, he and some chums were arrested for armed robbery—a monumentally dumb attempt that went sour because the Bakersfield bar they were robbing wasn't closed for the holiday, being as the holiday was actually the *next* day, and instead was full of customers, half of whom recognized them. So as Elvis rode the top of the charts, sharing space with newcomers Jerry Lee Lewis and the Everly Brothers, Merle was headed for thirty-three months (the maximum would have been fifteen years) in solitary at San Quentin— the "big house" itself.

It was a concert that Johnny Cash gave for the inmates there that inspired Merle to take up music as a vocation—how ironic that Merle served hard time while Johnny talked the talk (but we'll get to that later). When Merle was released in 1960, he went back to Bakersfield and dug ditches for $12 a day. He also washed dishes, laid pipe, and drove a truck. After all, a twenty-three-year-old ex-con couldn't expect to break into the business right away. But the music came along, slowly but surely, as Merle played in local bars and honed his skills.

In 1965, he had his first hit, the enduring "All My Friends Are Gonna Be Strangers," and broke into the C&W Top Ten with "Swinging Doors." He was named the New Male Vocalist of the Year and (with Bonnie Owens, Buck's former wife and Merle's new one) Vocal Duet of the Year by the Los Angeles–based Academy

Opposite: Merle performing at Tramps, New York City, June 1993. Above: San Quentin Prison, where Merle did hard time for thirty-three months after robbing a bar in Bakersfield, California.

Above: Johnny Cash gave legendary concerts at "big houses" like San Quentin and Folsom Prison, where the inmates related to his rough-hewn persona. But Cash never spent a day "inside the walls" himself—unlike his peers Merle Haggard and Johnny Paycheck. Opposite: Poet Rod McKuen appraises the stoic Merle Haggard in the cinema classic From Nashville with Music, a 1969 film that capitalized on Merle's huge hit "(I'm Proud to Be an) Okie from Muskogee."

of Country Music (ACM). In 1966 he had his first number-one hit, "I'm a Lonesome Fugitive." He then displaced fellow Bakersfield native Buck Owens as the ACM's Male Vocalist of the Year, and he and Bonnie again won the Vocal Duet award (as they also would in 1967). Merle had arrived.

He topped the C&W charts in 1967 and 1968 with self-penned odes to lawlessness like "The Fugitive," "Mama Tried," "Branded Man," and "The Legend of Bonnie and Clyde," making no bones about his firsthand knowledge of the California penal system or his intent to remain—symbolically, anyway—an outlaw. (Of course, being an ex-con hasn't had much of a stigma in country music anyway, what with half the male stars having served a little time here or there along the way.)

But Merle's years in the joint hadn't squeezed all the wildness out of his system by a long shot. As he toured with his award-winning band, The Strangers, Merle often found himself topping off a performance with an altercation or two. "Our music makes you want to either fuck or fight, just like Bob Wills' used to do," was his canny analysis of his appeal.

Sometimes his music waived the first part of the equation and proceeded directly to the second. "(I'm Proud to Be an) Okie from Muskogee," one of his three number-one hits from 1969, was a patriotic anthem that protested the rising tide of hippiedom. It was the cheery side of that year's hit film *Easy Rider*, which climaxes with one of the heroes getting his head blown off by a redneck in a pickup truck for flipping him the bird. (And it should be noted that Merle's dad grew up about twenty miles [32km] south of Muskogee before moving to California.) That year, the ACM named Merle Male Vocalist of the Year, with "Okie" winning Single of the Year, Song of the Year, and Album of the

Year. (Nashville's Country Music Association [CMA] gave Merle and "Okie" all those awards in 1970 instead.) But the true import of the song could be measured by the fact that President Nixon sent him a letter of congratulations and presidential cancidate George Wallace asked for Merle's endorsement. He declined.

Not many songs could polarize an audience like "Okie," but Merle wasn't through trying. (If George Jones was country's poet laureate of self-pity, Merle was the crown prince of pugnacity.) "The Fightin' Side of Me," his follow-up to "Okie," took the latter's "love it or leave it" sentiments and also went gold in 1970. There were more chart-toppers, many of which had socially conscious and/or autobiographical themes: "If

We Make It Through December" (about his failing marriage), "Kentucky Gambler" (Merle was a major-league gambler, winning and losing hundreds of thousands of dollars), "I Wonder If They Ever Think of Me" (about the POWs in Vietnam), "Hungry Eyes" (about the poor labor-camp workers he grew up with outside Bakersfield), "Workin' Man Blues," and "It's Not Love (But It's Not Bad)." "Always Wanting You" was a frank expression of his infatuation with Dolly Parton—one that, to his dismay, was never requited.

No doubt Merle was moved when then–Governor of California Ronald Reagan pardoned him in 1972 (nice try, Ron, but the time had already been served in full). But wife Bonnie Owens was much less

forgiving of his indiscretions (most of which he claimed not to remember in his 1981 autobiography, *Sing Me Back Home*), and she divorced him in 1976. Two years later he married band member Leona Williams—she had been one of those indiscretions—and Bonnie proved to be a good sport by serving as a bridesmaid. But those were hard years for Merle—he referred to the period as "male menopause"—and he retired from the business in 1979 to take stock of himself and where he was going.

Almost two years later he reemerged with a new enthusiasm, kicking off his comeback with his first chart-topper in five years, "I Think I'll Just Stay Here and Drink." He teamed up with George Jones in 1982 for a duet album, which yielded the number-one hit "Yesterday's Wine," and also recorded an album with Willie Nelson, *Pancho and Lefty*, for which the CMA voted them Vocal Duo of the Year in 1983. Leona divorced him that year, but Merle showed that he could also be a good sport by recording her song "Someday When Things Are Good," which hit number one. He won his first Grammy in 1984 for his song "That's the Way Love Goes," and "Natural High" (1985) and "Twinkle, Twinkle, Lucky Star" (1988) proved he could keep up with the new-wave stars of country.

Merle was named a "Living Legend" by The Nashville Network in 1990—the sort of award they give to someone who they figure is on the cusp of retirement. But Merle stormed back with the great album *1994*, an unqualified success that included neoclassics like "What's New in New York City," "Ramblin' Fever," and the hilariously politically incorrect "Set My Chickens Free"—demonstrating yet again that ex-cons from Bakersfield don't need no awards. Never did.

Hank Williams, Jr.
TOO ROWDY TO DIE

If Elvis had had a son, how hard would it now be for him to follow in his daddy's footsteps as a rock 'n' roll star? What sort of pressure would he find bearing down on him each and every day? To what microscopic scrutiny would he be subjected each time he stepped up to a microphone—and each time he stepped away from it? How could he ever live up to a legend? Would he die trying?

Those were the very problems that faced the son of Hank Williams, little "Bocephus," who was born in 1949 at the peak of his father's success, and only three when they found his father dead in the backseat of his Cadillac. While he may have been too young to really know or even remember his father, Hank, Jr., has spent the last forty-odd years waking and sleeping in the man's shadow. Small wonder that at various points he has attempted suicide, had a nervous breakdown, been

Hank Williams, Jr.—clean-cut and eager to please in this midsixties shot— was a tormented young man who nearly suffocated in the shadow of his legendary father.

hospitalized, and washed down a trainload of pills with an ocean of Jim Beam. The only wonder is that he has survived to become a superstar himself.

As soon as he could hold a little guitar, Hank, Jr., was trotted out on stage by his mommy, Hank's ex-wife, Audrey. Divorced from Hank in 1952, Audrey was hardly your typical mom—she was a hard-drinking, hard-hearted, ambitious woman who saw in her son a way to cash in on Hank's legacy after her own recording aspirations went bust. She trained Hank, Jr., to be a clone of his father, and at age eight he was lip-synching (and later singing) Hank's songs—and even mimicking his between-songs patter and jokes—on her Caravan of Stars tour in 1957, backed by Hank's old band, the Cheatin' Hearts. Performing since his debut in Swainsboro, Georgia, Hank, Jr., took the stage of the Grand Ole Opry for the first time when he was eleven. When Red Foley told him after one performance that he was nothing but the ghost of Hank, Sr., the youngster probably took it as a compliment. It might have even been intended as one.

Schooled in music by some of the greats—including Fats Domino and Earl Scruggs—Hank, Jr., soon displayed a considerable amount of his own talent. But that was sublimated by his mother and his manager, who were making a nice living by his ability to keep the Hank, Sr., franchise generating dollars. That was never more obvious than in 1964, when fifteen-year-old Hank, Jr., was hired by MGM to provide the soundtrack for the film the studio was making about his dad's life, *Your Cheatin' Heart.* Hank re-created the songs note for note—just as he'd been programmed to do—while star George Hamilton, Jr., lip-synched them. And why not? Hank had already recorded albums like *Songs My Father Left Me* and *Hank Williams, Jr. Sings the Songs of Hank Williams.*

Here's Hank, Jr., as he appears today, bullet-studded guitar strap and all.

But someone must have forgotten to put enough coins in young Hank, because as he grew into his teens he became less and less content to perform as a windup doll. "There's no doubt I was haunted by Daddy," he later reflected. "I used to cry all the time, sitting in front of a record player listening to his records with the biggest bottle of Jim Beam I could find, trying to communicate with him." This disquiet began to be reflected in his music; one of his first Top Ten hits was "Standin' in the Shadows (of a Very Famous Man)." By the time he was twenty-one, he'd started to remove himself from that shadow. His songs "All for the Love of Sunshine" and "Eleven Roses" both hit number one, and neither sounded the least bit like his dad. But they didn't sound like the real Hank, Jr., either.

Frustrated by his lack of musical progress, Hank turned to those old Nashville standbys, pills and alcohol. He absorbed them like a sponge, but few noticed.

Hank, Jr., may have lost his shirt here, but he somehow found the strength to say goodbye to cocaine, a decision that probably saved his life. Incidentally, even his legendary daddy never mastered playing the fiddle.

Substance abuse was a congenital hazard of the business, and Hank wasn't doing anything that his fellow performers weren't doing—although *they* weren't haunted by the shadow of the biggest star who'd ever walked on the Opry's stage. Weighed down by that legacy, he put the pedal to the metal and tried to speed up his trip to the pearly gates. In 1973, he wound up having his stomach pumped at a Nashville hospital after he'd taken an overdose of barbiturates. Hank, Sr., had died at twenty-nine, and at twenty-four, Hank, Jr., seemed bent on beating him to the finish line. "Taking a bottle of Darvon and getting pumped out is not fun," he sagely observed after that close call.

Warned by psychiatrists that he was harboring a death wish—again, par for the course in Nashville—a defiant Hank moved to Alabama and recorded an album, *Hank Williams, Jr. and Friends*, with a rowdy, Louisiana-bayou flavor that expressed the new musical direction he wanted to take. While waiting for the album's release (which took nearly a year, because of legal complications), Hank took a vacation in August 1975 at Montana's Mount Ajax. Standing on a ledge at an elevation of nine thousand feet (2,700m), Hank slipped, falling five hundred feet (150m) and crashing face-first into a boulder that nearly tore him in half. His teeth were knocked out, his skull was split open, his nose was missing in action, and one eye socket was shattered. It took nine operations and over a year of recuperation to put the pieces back together. "The doctors told me later that they'd expected me to die," Hank reflected. He didn't, obviously, but his face would never look the same again.

Nor would his music ever sound the same. Perhaps those near-death experiences had finally freed him from the shackles of being Hank Williams' only son. (Audrey's death during his recuperation may not have hurt either, although he would never admit as much.) With the support of his wife-to-be, Becky, he plunged into shaping his new sound and new career. With the help of Waylon Jennings, who served as producer, he cut the album *The New South* in 1977, a bold departure artistically. But if the record signaled the new leaf he had turned over, some things remained the same: Hank was hospitalized three times within a year for near-fatal overdoses of cocaine, and also blasted a number of hotel rooms into oblivion with his cherished firearms.

What may have saved Hank from himself was the success of his next album, *Family Tradition*, in 1979. Its kick-ass title song humorously—and without a trace of self-pity—admitted the connection between the self-destructive way he was living his life and the way Hank, Sr., had lived his. Somehow the recording took the onus off those who had felt sorry for him. One of the album's cuts, "Texas Women," gave him his first number-one hit in nine years. Next came the 1981 *Whiskey Bent and Hell-Bound* album, with its number-one hit "All My Rowdy Friends (Have Settled Down)" and the defiant anthem "A Country Boy Can Survive." It helped that he had sworn off the cocaine (but not the whiskey). As he so succinctly put it, "Sex feels good, Jim Beam tastes good, but cocaine will kill your ass."

Free of his demons at last, Bocephus has felt confident enough to record a number of Hank, Sr.'s most popular songs, even hitting the top of the charts with his remakes of "Honky Tonkin'" and "Mind Your Own Business." In fact, he even "dueted" with Hank, Sr., in 1989 with the record and video of "There's a Tear in My Beer." Hank, Jr., had come across an old kinescope of his dad performing and joined him onstage, thanks to the wonders of technology (creepy in a way, but also touching). The ACM voted him Entertainer of the Year in 1986 and 1987, and the CMA seconded the honor

in 1987 and 1988, as if heaping on the honors now could make reparation for twenty years of being ignored and ostracized. Well—maybe it did.

Hank has also been sidetracked the last several years with court activity initiated by his half-sister, Cathy Stone (who now performs as Jett Williams). Born to Hank, Sr., and Bobbie Webb Jett out of wedlock in 1952, Stone has been suing for a share of the estate for nearly a decade. While that matter drags on, Hank still performs, though his once-legendary concerts and rabble-rousing recordings have been less than inspired of late. (The theme song he composed and performed for ABC-TV's *Monday Night Football* a few years back was great, however.) Has the Rowdy One himself settled down for good? Or is this the calm before another storm? We shall see.

a country boy can survive. Bocephus certainly has served his own kind of hard time, looking death right in the eye and then walking away. That puts him one up on Hank, Sr. Here, Hank, Jr., sings the theme song he penned for ABC's **Monday Night Football** *a few years ago.*

TAMMY
WYNETTE

LORETTA
LYNN

DOLLY
PARTON

Your Good Girl's Gonna Go Bad

Tammy Wynette

THE DOYENNE
OF D-I-V-O-R-C-E

She may have started as Virginia Wynette Pugh on a farm in Itawamba County, Mississippi, in 1942, but it was as Tammy Wynette—a name conjured up by brilliant producer Billy Sherrill—that the world came to know and, yes, love her. As much as any country singer before her or since, Tammy Wynette seemed to live the epically unhappy life she sang about so plaintively. Despite any number of triumphs on the recording front, she was a born victim, much like the protagonists of her tear-jerking songs.

Raised by a blind father who would not live to celebrate her first birthday and a mother who implemented her dying husband's wish that young Virginia should learn to sing and play the attic full of instruments he would be leaving behind, Virginia grew up picking cotton, singing along with country stars over the radio, and practicing the guitar, flute, piano, organ, and accordion. But in an effort to establish her independence, she dropped out of high school at seventeen to marry an oft-unemployed construction worker named Euple Byrd; the name alone should have tipped her off that the guy was a loser.

Euple promptly moved Virginia into a drafty log cabin that she tried to improve by tearing up cardboard boxes and nailing them over the chinks as insulation. They had two daughters together, but life became more and more of a struggle for Virginia, and in 1964, at twenty-two, she suffered a full-fledged nervous breakdown due to the accumulation of various pressures. In the hospital, she endured electroshock therapy along

It's a long, long way from Birmingham's Midfield Beauty Salon to gold records, movie soundtracks, and mantels full of Grammy Awards, but Tammy Wynette has made that journey.

Tammy with Merle Haggard at the Country Music
Awards in October 1991.

that also employed her uncle, it turned out: Eddie Burns, the host of the local television program *The Country Boy Eddie Show*. She was such a success that Eddie, who could only pay her $35 a week, urged her to try her luck in Nashville. And even though Virginia hadn't had much luck through the first twenty-three years of her life, she took his advice and commuted between Birmingham and her base in Nashville, the Anchor Inn Motel.

Her simple goal was to be granted an audition, but the usual string of rejections was her reward. (She did win a consolation prize of sorts, though, when she married a clerk at her motel, Don Chapel, in 1965 [Virginia's judgment, or lack thereof, might have had something to do with her lifelong streak of misfortune].) But she was introduced to Porter Wagoner, who hired her to tour with him for a week. That minor break helped her get in Billy Sherrill's door; Sherrill politely listened to her sing and told her he'd get back to her. The amazing thing was, he did.

Sherrill had a tune in hand called "Apartment #9," penned by an aspiring singer named Johnny Paycheck, which he thought would be perfect for Virginia's tearstained style. But that name—! He respectfully suggested she lose the Pugh, use Wynette as her last name, and call herself Tammy. Agreeable as always, Tammy saw her very first record make the Top Twenty. Her next release, "Your Good Girl's Gonna Go Bad," went all the way to number three. Sherrill cannily teamed her with David Houston for the great tune "My Elusive Dreams," which hit number one in September 1967. Sherrill and Glenn Sutton wrote "I Don't Wanna Play House (No More)," which won her a Grammy, and followed that by composing "Take Me to Your World," which became her first solo number-

with the knowledge that she was pregnant again. When she finally recovered, Virginia declared the marriage over and—despite her mother's objections—moved with her daughters to Birmingham, where a kindly aunt and uncle took them in. She labored as a beautician at the Midfield Beauty Salon until the day her third daughter, Tina, arrived a few months prematurely, afflicted with spinal meningitis.

Virginia didn't earn enough to cover Tina's medical bills, and she knew she had to make some extra money. Being hired to sing would be a wonderful way out of her bind—but what philanthropist would employ a divorcée with no performing experience? One

one hit. She'd have another chart-topper in June 1968, the now-classic "D-I-V-O-R-C-E," of which she later commented, "It went right along with my life."

Yes, her marriage to erstwhile motel clerk Don Chapel was on the rocks, and once again it was Tammy calling the shots. Now one of the most successful singers in her field, she had finally met lifelong idol George Jones on equal ground, and the two took to each other in a big way—so big, that Chapel was down for the count even as "D-I-V-O-R-C-E" was riding the top of the country charts; so big, that Chapel slapped Jones with a $100,000 alienation of affection suit as soon as the divorce papers were served (they settled out of court). Tammy and George were married on February 25, 1969, in Ringgold, Georgia, although they had announced their marriage in 1968 to forestall questions about their living together at George's Lakeland, Florida, theme park. "Very few people get to marry their idol," she proudly boasted. "I did."

For a few years life was paradise, with Tammy savoring three consecutive Female Vocalist of the Year awards from the CMA in 1968, 1969, and 1970, and a Grammy Award for "Stand by Your Man," which she wrote with Sherrill and the song with which she will always be identified. She also earned the distinction of having five of her songs used on the soundtrack of the

The erstwhile Virginia Wynette Pugh—better known to her fans as Tammy Wynette—got her fondest wish in the person of her idol, George Jones, whom she married once and nearly divorced a hundred times, and who finally broke her heart for good.

lauded 1970 film *Five Easy Pieces*. And the happy couple had a daughter named (with the wisdom of Solomon) Tamala Georgette.

But Jones had always been a heavy drinker, and this bout with matrimony somehow intensified the urge. By August 1973 paradise had been lost, with George's booze-soaked, ten-day vanishing act precipitating divorce proceedings by Tammy. The couple reconciled a month later, even recording a duet to commemorate the event, "We're Gonna Hold On." "I

Tamala Georgette Jones, daughter of George Jones and Tammy Wynette, shares a moment with her proud papa onstage.

wouldn't live without him; I just couldn't," she told the press. But two months later she decided she could, after George walked out on her again. This time the divorce took, and so did Tammy. She took the house, their twelve-bunk touring bus (with "Mr. & Mrs. Country Music" painted on its side), and even George's band, the Jones Boys, which she renamed the Country Gentlemen.

Incredibly, despite all the bad blood, George and Tammy continued to record duets (like the number-one hit "Near You"), singing together even while refusing to speak. "He nipped and I nagged," she explained of their dissolution. The rest of George's story is told elsewhere in this volume, but for Tammy the single life wasn't all bad. She dated a professional football player and one of the Gatlin brothers, then had an affair with Burt Reynolds that probably counted as her biggest crossover hit. But when she couldn't rope Reynolds down permanently, she married a real-estate tycoon named Michael Tomlin on the rebound. This time the union lasted all of forty-four days. In 1978 she walked down the aisle again, this time with Jones' old pal George Richey, a songwriter who had divorced his wife, Sheila, to be with Tammy. She now had a mansion with fifteen bathrooms—a better status symbol in Nashville than a whole fleet of Cadillacs.

Tammy decided to pen her autobiography, *Stand by Your Man*, published in 1979 (and filmed two years later as a pretty good television movie, with Annette O'Toole as Tammy). But she had written the story of her life prematurely; in fact, very little would happen of a positive nature, professionally or otherwise, from there on. First her mansion was nearly burned down in an act of arson that was never solved. Then Tammy was abducted at gunpoint from a Nashville parking lot. She was driven to a secluded area, beaten, and left with a pair of pantyhose tied tightly around her neck. Later she intimated that she knew who had been

Tammy today, showing the wear and tear of a very tough life. But after all the miseries and near-death experiences, she still has a voice that could launch a thousand ships.

behind it, but the attack remained a mystery—and some hinted that it had all been staged for the publicity (her career had been skidding).

Her love life had long been a disaster area, but in the early eighties, Tammy entered a phase of health crises that would have given pause to Camille. She had already been hospitalized for a kidney infection, as well as the aforementioned premature birth and nervous breakdown. Now, in rapid succession, came a hysterectomy, a gallbladder removal, and the excision of sev-

eral feet of infected intestines. After nearly twenty operations, she found herself addicted to painkillers and, in 1986, had to check into the Betty Ford Center for rehabilitation. By 1988 she regained her health, but a bad real estate investment forced her and George Richey to file for bankruptcy. On top of that, her daughter Tina appeared to be turning into a full-fledged juvenile delinquent. Through it all, Tammy continued to perform. But now she simply wasn't strong enough. She twice collapsed onstage in Australia in 1992, then had half her stomach removed when her remaining intestines became infected again. Yet, she forged on.

In 1992 she had a surprise international hit with the folk-flavored "Justified and Ancient," recorded with the English dance-band KLF; the song went to number one in an astonishing eighteen countries. With that newly minted credibility putting Tammy back square in the public eye, Epic released *Tears of Fire*, a deluxe "25th Anniversary Collection" of Tammy's music—sixty-seven songs that amount to more than three hours of playing time.

Suddenly, Tammy was no longer just a page out of history. She began recording an album of duets with Tom Petty, Elton John, and Bonnie Raitt, as well as the *Honky Tonk Angels* album, a 1993 collaboration with Dolly Parton and Loretta Lynn that combined new songs like "Keep It, You Can Call It a Memory" with standards like "Silver Threads and Golden Needles." To celebrate, she and George moved into Hank Williams' old mansion. "I'm putting in a hot-pink beauty shop," she explained in a 1992 interview with *Country Music* magazine. "All my appliances from the beauty shop are hot pink." And we know, Hank would've wanted it that way.

Loretta Lynn

NOT A
HONKY-TONK GIRL

Married at thirteen, mother of four at eighteen, a star at twenty-five, and a grandmother at thirty-six, Loretta Lynn has always lived her life twice as fast as anyone else. But even though she has attained a level of success shared by few of country music's women, this nightingale has been plagued by more misfortunes than Pharaoh down in Egypt-land. She has been the victim of car accidents, bleeding ulcers, and blood poisoning and other infections. She has undergone breast surgery and has been stricken by endless migraine attacks and uncountable collapses due to stress and exhaustion. And that's not counting her addiction to painkillers, and at least one suicide attempt. As for her claims to psychic powers, her previous lives as an Indian princess and a galley maid, and her palmreading abilities—well, who knows? But there are those who maintain that she's been about three bricks shy of a load for quite some time.

Born in Butcher Hollow in eastern Kentucky's coal-mining country on April 14, 1935, Loretta Webb (named after movie star Loretta Young) would have had to strike gold just to advance to the level of simple poverty. The second of eight children, she watched her father, Teddy Webb, work in the Van Lear coal mines until he had gotten the black lung, then dropped out of the eighth grade to marry Mooney Doolittle (né Oliver) Lynn, a nineteen-year-old World War II veteran who swept her off her feet at a school dance. By the time she was eighteen, the couple had moved to Washington state, and it was there that "Doo," as she called her husband when they were getting along, encouraged her to learn the guitar, write songs, and sing.

After much urging from Doo, she began playing in public; little sister Crystal Gayle had been performing on the radio for years before Loretta took up the cause at the advanced age of twenty-four. Her band, the Trail Blazers, attracted enough of a local following to earn them a spot on Buck Owens' Tacoma-based television show. In 1960 she cut her first record, "I'm a Honky Tonk Girl." As immortalized in the 1980 film about her life, *Coal Miner's Daughter*, Loretta and Doo promoted the song tirelessly, traveling from coast to coast visiting country radio stations, figuring her per-

A recent photograph of Loretta and her husband, *Mooney Doolittle Lynn. Loretta dropped out of the eighth grade to marry the then-nineteen-year-old, whom she met at a school dance. Sissy Spacek and Tommy Lee Jones portrayed the couple in the Oscar-nominated film* Coal Miner's Daughter.

sonal appearance would inspire more airplay. The strategy worked, and by the end of the year she had been invited to appear on the *Opry*.

That exposure helped her records break into the Top Ten, but it took her until 1966 to score her first chart-topper, the no-nonsense "Don't Come Home A-Drinkin' (With Lovin' on Your Mind)." There wasn't much nonsense in her number-one follow-up "Fist City," either; it was directed at a Nashville woman who'd been hitting on Doo in clubs while Loretta was performing onstage. (Her earlier hit "You Ain't Woman Enough [To Take My Man]" may have had the same inspiration—Doo fancied himself a ladies' man in those days.) As the hits kept coming through the sixties and into the seventies, she vied with Tammy Wynette for the throne unofficially awarded to country's queen. Loretta was named the top Female Vocalist in the first CMA awards, but Tammy won the Grammy for Best Song of the Year and would win most of the awards for the next few years.

But "You've Just Stepped in (From Steppin' Out on Me)," "Your Squaw Is on the Warpath," and "Woman of the World (Leave My World Alone)" exemplified Loretta's feisty weltanschauung, so different from Tammy's hermetically sealed masochism, and Loretta's triumphal autobiographical song "Coal Miner's Daughter" made it to number one just before Christmas, 1970. (The title served her well again for the memoir she penned with George Vecsey, which became a best-seller.) Loretta then had the masterstroke of teaming up with Conway Twitty, with their 1971 "After the Fire Is Gone" inaugurating a wildly successful string of duets—just one per year, thank you ma'am—that made them country's most popular duo of the decade.

Always happy to engage controversy, she had a number-one song with "One's on the Way," a riotous ode to the joys of multiple motherhood; Loretta was

Loretta Lynn and Conway Twitty were country music's top award-winning duo in 1971.

well versed in the topic, having had four kids by the age of eighteen and twins just a year before at the age of thirty-five. That tune and others like "You're Lookin' at Country" helped her win the CMA's perfecta for 1972, being named both top Female Vocalist and Entertainer of the Year. She was the first woman to be so much as *nominated* for the Entertainer award—no surprise in Nashville's antediluvian patriarchy—and her win turned the town upside-down. "Louisiana Woman, Mississippi Man" led to another CMA award for Loretta and Conway as the top Vocal Duo of 1973; they also nailed down the award in 1974 and 1975, and might have kept going if Waylon Jennings and Willie Nelson hadn't decided to record as a team.

Loretta, flanked by her mother and sister Crystal Gayle, picks up the ACM award for Artist of the Decade in 1980. The remainder of the decade proved to be less kind to Loretta than the seventies, when she reigned as country music's queen.

But even as her career was peaking professionally, Loretta was being dragged down by a whirlpool of troubles. She was hospitalized for exhaustion nine times in 1972 alone, even passing out onstage on more than one occasion. (That tendency was "quoted" by the Ronee Blakely character in Robert Altman's 1975 film *Nashville*; Loretta's habit of launching into long, rambling, incoherent monologues while onstage was also captured by Blakely and Altman.) "I just go into sort of a coma," Loretta explained at the time. "Just pass out, when I don't even know it's coming on." She also suffered from bleeding ulcers and chronic migraines, which became so intense they'd make her vomit.

But that wasn't the worst of it. Around the time *Nashville* came out, she began taking—and abusing—antidepressants and painkillers, finally earning a stint

in Nashville's Park View Hospital after an accidental overdose. "Every time I felt nervous I'd take a pill. It got to where if I started crying I'd take one," she confessed in a 1977 interview with *Esquire*. "If I was still shaking, I'd take two. Finally it got to where things were so bad I'd just take some Librium and go to sleep." She told a *Rolling Stone* reporter that she felt as depressed as Marilyn Monroe must have been. "Too many responsibilities, too many conflicts, too much guilt," she explained. "I think I'm one of the unhappiest people in the world. 'Bout half the time I cry myself to sleep." Little wonder she made an attempt at suicide, holding her pearl-handled revolver to her head one day when the agony of a migraine attack made her think about ending it all. "I didn't want to kill myself," she told her doctor. "I just wanted to kill the pain."

It was around this time that she scandalized Nashville by confessing she had turned her back on the teachings of the Church of Christ and accepted the fact that she was reincarnated from a number of past lives. Loretta began holding seances at her house, trying to delve into her history. In one past life, she was an Indian princess named Little Flower. In another, she was an Irish servant girl having an affair with King George, whose best friend ended up choking her to death. (Now, *that's* depressing.) She also professed to have had psychic powers since the age of nineteen. "I look at someone's eyes and I know what's coming. People would say I was crazy if they knew the things I do." And a lot of them did say she was crazy—not that Loretta cared much.

Little sister Crystal Gayle had earned her own share of the spotlight with her Grammy-winning "Don't It Make My Brown Eyes Blue" in 1977, and Loretta was spurred by her sister's achievement to return her attention to songwriting and recording. She had a number-one hit with the appropriately titled "Out of My Head and Back in Bed," and was voted the Artist of the Decade by the ACM in 1980. But that honor was overshadowed by the triumph of the film version of *Coal Miner's Daughter*, which was nominated for a passel of Oscars in 1980, including the one Sissy Spacek won as Best Actress. The film's success gave Loretta a cachet far beyond that enjoyed by any of country music's other female royalty—Crystal, Dolly, and Tammy couldn't point to a similar achievement. But Loretta was still Loretta. When asked by *The New York Times* whether the film was an accurate portrayal of her life, she replied candidly, "If the movie had told everything, there'd have been about fifty hours of fighting."

The accidental drowning death of her beloved son, Jack, in 1984 (he fell from a horse while trying to ford a river) took some of the vinegar out of her, but nothing seems likely to stop Loretta entirely. "Death doesn't end things," she wrote in her autobiography. "I think we keep on goin' till we get it right." In 1988, she was voted into the Country Hall of Fame and elected to the Nashville Songwriter Association's Hall of Fame. Most recently, she was in fine form on the *Honky Tonk Angels* album with Dolly Parton and Tammy Wynette—her onetime rivals for the throne—which included their stirring renditions of such C&W classics as "Lovesick Blues" and "It Wasn't God Who Made Honky Tonk Angels."

The Most Poetic C&W Song Titles

"All My Ex's Live in Texas"

"If I Said You Had a Beautiful Body (Would You Hold It Against Me?)"

"She's Actin' Single (I'm Drinking Doubles)"

"Don't Wipe the Tears that You Cry for Him on My Good White Shirt"

"He's Got Nothing on Me but You"

"Stand on My Own Two Knees"

"Get Your Biscuits in the Oven and Your Buns in Bed"

"I Don't Mind the Thorns (If You're the Rose)"

"Old Flames Can't Hold a Candle to You"

"Sleeping Single in a Double Bed"

"It's Not Love (But It's Not Bad)"

"I Think I'll Just Stay Here and Drink"

"She Left Love All Over Me"

"I'm Gonna Hire a Wino to Decorate Our Home"

"She Got the Gold Mine (I Got the Shaft)"

"Let's Chase Each Other Around the Room"

"Heaven's Just a Sin Away"

Dolly Parton

HOLLYWOOD, DOLLYWOOD, SCHMOLLYWOOD

"It takes a lot of money to make me look this cheap," Dolly Parton once cracked. But if her zaftig presence has been the butt of several acres' worth of bad jokes, Dolly has always been the first to provide a punch line. "I look like the girl next door," she once deadpanned, "if you happen to live next door to an amusement park." Sense of humor aside, she has been country music's biggest (no pun intended) female star for the better part of twenty years—the Barbra Streisand of the rhinestones 'n' jeans crowd with a multimedia presence that most country performers can only dream about. But the long road to this summit was not paved with gold—or even paved!—and a myriad of conflicts between her career and rather mysterious love life have dogged her along the way.

Like most country singers who have managed to make it big, Dolly Rebecca Parton was obsessed at an early age with becoming a star. Born on January 19, 1946, on a dirt-poor farm in Locust, Tennessee, she was the fourth of what would eventually be twelve children. Getting her hands on a used mandolin when she was six, she taught herself to play and was composing her own songs almost before she learned to spell. By the time she was ten she was already a veteran of radio and television shows in nearby Knoxville, and she made her *Opry* debut at the tender age of twelve.

Actually, there wasn't much that was tender about Dolly except her age. Early on, she seemed to sense what it would take to get to the top, and she went after it like a bulldozer goes after a hill. The minute she graduated from high school in 1964, she

was off to Nashville, peddling her songs (Hank Williams, Jr., had a hit with "I'm in No Condition") and waiting for someone to give the demure mountain flower with the Jackie Kennedy hairdo a shot in a recording studio. In 1967 someone did, and the result was the minor hit "Dumb Blonde," the irony of which was surely lost on straitlaced Nashville. (As Dolly has since remarked, "I'm not offended by all the dumb-blonde jokes, because I know I'm not dumb—and I also know I'm not blonde!")

That hit was enough to bring her to the attention of Porter Wagoner, who hired her that October to join

Opposite: Dolly performing in the late eighties. Above: Dolly Parton and Porter Wagoner put on a happy face for the camera. Their 1974 split was one of the most bitter disputes Nashville had witnessed in many a moon. In the late seventies, the two settled out of court, with Porter collecting a lot of money, thanks to a contract that guaranteed him a percentage of Dolly's income as her "producer."

his syndicated television show, *The Porter Wagoner Show*, replacing his longtime "girl singer" Norma Jean, who'd up and left. Over the next several years Porter and Dolly would enjoy spectacular success, with a record (for a duo) fourteen Top Ten hits on the C&W charts, including "The Last Thing on My Mind," "If Teardrops Were Pennies," and "Just Someone I Used to Know." But Dolly—always ambitious—had also been pursuing her solo career. She'd gotten a contract with RCA thanks to Porter's help, and had a number of

hits of her own, with "Mule Skinner Blues" becoming her first Top Ten hit in 1970, and "Joshua" her first number-one tune in 1971.

By 1974, when "Jolene" became her second chart-topper, Dolly was already planning her split from Porter. Not surprisingly, she found him to be mighty angry about it, feeling that he'd made her what she was and that she was an ungrateful so-and-so. It was a classic *A Star Is Born* scenario, with Dolly's star ascending in direct proportion to Porter's waning one. At first he made gallant noises in public about the split, issuing this generous statement at their February 1974 press conference: "Dolly is now a superstar in every way; she's well prepared to go on her own." But after he'd marinated for a time in the juices of envy, he began to whistle a different tune. "Dolly didn't quit me," he insisted in a pique of revisionist history. "I let her go. I gave her notice in Tulsa that she couldn't stay. I wasn't going to travel with a girl I had to fight with on the road." Ironically, their duet "Please Don't Stop Loving Me" hit number one in the midst of the fracas.

The split took a nasty turn when Porter sued her for breach of contract in 1979. By now Dolly was very big indeed, having had a string of number-one hits ("Love Is Like a Butterfly," "The Bargain Store") and been named Female Vocalist of the Year by the CMA in 1975 and 1976 and Entertainer of the Year in 1977 and 1978 by the ACM. She'd also had her first crossover hits, "Here You Come Again" and "Heartbreaker," both calculated attempts to widen her fan base to include the pop market—a career move that angered much of Nashville, which still was irked at Dolly's move to Los Angeles management the year before. But the move worked, even winning her a Grammy for her *Here You Come Again* album in 1978.

So Porter wasn't just taking on some "girl singer" with that lawsuit; now he was threatening an institution (one whose most recent album was called,

The pre–Rhinestone Cowgirl. Dolly performs on an acoustic guitar on The Porter Wagoner Show *in the late sixties.*

fittingly, *Great Balls of Fire*). He wanted the staggering sum of $3 million on the grounds that the contract she'd signed with him back in 1970 guaranteeing him a percentage of her income as "producer" was still in effect. Their battle polarized Nashville, half of which was still miffed at Dolly for "selling out" and "going pop"; the other half heard Porter's complaints as an advanced case of sour grapes and greed. But before the year was out, Dolly agreed to settle out of court with him, essentially giving him half her income since first joining him in 1967, and taking half his income over the same period. That cost Dolly big-time—her fees had jumped to $30,000 a night by now, the kind of money Porter would never see—but she was free and clear at last.

Or was she? When portions of Porter's self-suppressed autobiography were published in the tabloids, his revelation that the two had been lovers during their early years together linked them in the headlines again. Since Dolly had been married since 1966 to building contractor Carl Dean, this wasn't the best sort of public relations. Dolly maintained that there'd always been at least a microphone stand between her and Porter (although she did once teasingly admit in a *Playboy* interview, "If I wanted to [have an extramarital affair], I would....Nothin's better than sex when you think you have to sneak it"). Rumors of an affair between her and Merle Haggard, with whom she'd toured for a spell, didn't help; neither did the fact that the enigmatic Carl Dean, whose ultralow profile makes Howard Hughes look like an exhibitionist, was never seen with her on the road.

As if to punctuate just how huge a star she now was, Dolly made her screen debut in the blockbuster feminist comedy *9 to 5* in 1980, turning in an accom-

Kenny Rogers and Dolly collect a couple of Grammys for their 1983 smash duet, "Islands in the Stream." Who'd have thought back in the sixties, when their respective careers started, that thirty years later they'd be two of pop music's biggest superstars?

plished performance as one of the exploited secretaries; costars Jane Fonda and Lily Tomlin had handpicked Dolly to be their third wheel. For good measure, Dolly also sang the best-selling theme song, which she wrote out of boredom while sitting on the set; it reached number one on both the C&W and pop charts in 1981 (the first country song to do so since "Harper Valley PTA" in 1967), and won a Grammy. Hollywood provided her with the cachet to play Las Vegas, and in February of that year she began headlining at the Riviera Hotel for a cool $250,000 per week.

It was fitting that Dolly's next project would be a screen adaptation of the Broadway musical *The Best Little Whorehouse in Texas*, since she had once admitted in a *Ladies Home Journal* interview: "I always liked the look of our hookers back home....Their big hairdos and makeup made them look *more*, [and] I go for more. When people say less is more, I say less is less." (Small wonder that she topped the list of Blackwell's Worst Dressed Celebrities in 1978!) *Best Little Whorehouse*, with its pedigree, big budget, and talented cast (including Burt Reynolds), was intended to be more, but it turned out to be less—which is to say, a mess. Not that Dolly didn't do justice to her part as Miss Mona, the brothel's bighearted madam. Just about its only highlight was her singing "I Will Always Love You," a number-one hit for her back in 1974, commemorating her split from Porter Wagoner; now it topped the charts again in this newly recorded version (as it would yet again for Whitney Houston in the 1992 film *The Bodyguard*, to become the only song in music history to hit number one three times).

This was also the year during which Dollywood, her four-hundred-acre (160ha) theme park, opened in Pigeon Forge, Tennessee, not so far from where she and her eleven siblings were raised. She was still an unstoppable force on the recording front, having gigantic hits with "Islands in the Stream," her 1983 duet with Kenny Rogers that went platinum, and her album *The Great Pretender*, a partially successful effort to revive rock 'n' roll classics like "Save the Last Dance for Me." But if Dolly was depressed at the poor reception to *Whorehouse*, she must have been suicidal about the jeers that greeted her next movie, the laughable *Rhinestone*, which was based on the song "Rhinestone Cowboy." Worse, whereas Burt Reynolds had been merely unconvincing in *Whorehouse*, Sylvester Stallone here was an abomination—so terrible that he even managed to make Dolly look bad. Anyway, she cried all the

way to the bank—her fee for the film had been $3 million, which presumably included the thirteen songs she composed for its soundtrack.

Dolly now seemed at times to be a parody of herself, even when she wasn't kidding around. Her mid-eighties television specials with Kenny Rogers contained some decent work, but her 1987 ABC-TV series *Dolly* was a $44 million (the amount ABC paid her) disaster, big-boob jokes and all. ("My daddy always said you shouldn't try to put fifty pounds of mud in a five-pound sack" was one of her best impromptu lines, generated after she spilled out of her dress at a CMA

Awards show.) Then there were the dramatic weight fluctuations, which took her from a robust 160 pounds (73kg) to the verge of anorexia nervosa, and back again—real meat for the tabloids, but not exactly the scandal of the century.

Of far more interest was the *Trio* album on which she, Emmylou Harris, and Linda Ronstadt had been laboring over off and on for nine years. Named 1987's top album by the ACM, it went gold and then platinum, yielded the number-one hit "To Know Him Is to Love Him," and won a Grammy. But Dolly's former ironfisted control of the charts weakened as the

nineties dawned, although *Eagle When She Flies* did go platinum, and her 1989 "roots" album *White Limozeen* (produced by Ricky Skaggs) went gold. As the Mary Chapin Carpenters, Kathy Matteas, and k.d. langs move onto her once-sacrosanct turf, Dolly now seems content to record now and then with other living legends like Tammy Wynette and Loretta Lynn, having the occasional spot of plastic surgery. (Dolly: it's not necessary!)

Films now seem to command most of her attention; Dollywood meets Hollywood, and Nashville snickers. (Still, she looked great in her black satin gown at the 1993 Academy Awards show!) With the right vehicle, though, her acting is no joke—she was fine in the 1989 *Steel Magnolias* as the operator of a beauty parlor in a small Louisiana town. On the other hand, she was an embarrassment in the 1992 bomb *Straight Talk*, in which she plays a Daisy Maeish hillbilly who accidentally becomes a Chicago radio-show psychologist, whose Tennessee-mountain homilies prove to be just what her big-city listeners need to straighten out their lives. (And James Woods, Mr. Psychopath himself, as a romantic interest? Dolly may be in need of a little career guidance.) But at least her new project, a television movie about an evangelist (tentatively titled *High and Mighty*), promises to play to her strengths. "It's not a heavy-duty religious experience," Dolly elaborated in a recent interview. "When I write them gospel songs, I get into it. I guess it's a chance to let everything out; all you hear, all your feelings." Her autobiography, *Dolly: My Life and Other Unfinished Business*, was unleashed with a first printing of one million copies late in 1994, indicating that Dollywood is becoming the world according to Dolly.

"Et tu, Brute?" Dolly wonders what possessed her to star opposite the unintelligible Sly Stallone in the 1984 megabomb Rhinestone. The Plot: he's a New York cab driver; she teaches him to sing C&W. Right!

JOHNNY CASH

GEORGE JONES

JOHNNY PAYCHECK

Doin' Time in a Honky-Tonk Prison

Johnny Cash

WALKING THE LINE

Unlike many country stars who do their darnedest to cover up the evil things they've done and the bad places they've been, Johnny Cash—he of the fifty million albums sold—has gone out of his way to encourage the notion that he's a notorious (albeit reformed) menace to society. Why? Because his grim but oh-so-exploitable "Man in Black" image is a boast that he's done it all and been everywhere; how else could he write a song like "Folsom Prison Blues"? In reality, though, Johnny Cash is guilty only of having been a major-league pill-popper whose past brushes with the law have been elevated into parlous deeds that rank with those of John Dillinger. But the one doing most of the mythologizing is Cash himself, who's about as dangerous to others as Mr. Peepers.

Born in 1932 in a government-founded farming community in Arkansas called Dyess, J.R. Cash (as his birth certificate read) was raised at the height of the Depression, picking cotton and dreaming of better times and places. He found a better place—sort of—when he enlisted in the Air Force as "John Cash" at the age of eighteen and was shipped over to Germany. He spent the next four years singing to the fräuleins and brawling with his fellow GIs (and sometimes vice versa), altering the topography of his face into its now familiar, battered form. When he was discharged he made his way to Memphis, married one Vivian Liberto, and tried to make a living as a door-to-door salesman. But with that puss, no doubt he was turned away more often than not. Since he wanted to be a singer anyway, Johnny didn't take the rejection personally; instead he used the GI Bill to get into radio announcer's school and trained to be a deejay.

With Luther Perkins and Marshall Grant—"The Tennessee Two"—Johnny began performing in and around Memphis. After considerable begging, the trio got a tryout with Sam Phillips of Sun Records, Elvis Presley's label. Phillips was about to sell Elvis to RCA for $40,000, so Johnny Cash sounded good to him. Cash's initial 1955 release, "Cry, Cry, Cry," was only a middling success, but "I Walk the Line" topped the country charts in 1956, and Johnny was on his way. Another 1956 hit, "Folsom Prison Blues," was inspired by a movie—not by any first-hand experience with Folsom, San Quentin, or any other prison (although Cash's 1968 version, recorded live at Folsom itself, helped reinforce that legend).

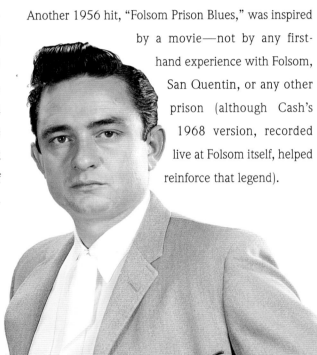

Now performing up to three hundred nights a year as Johnny Cash and the Tennessee Three, Cash understandably found his stamina in need of reinforcements. Dexedrine was but one of Johnny's little helpers, and downers and liquor helped him relax after the show. That roller coaster would fry anyone's circuits, and Cash once overdosed on his tour bus, nearly dying. He was a breakdown just waiting to happen—cracking up his cars, destroying hotel suites, appearing at shows too inebriated to perform, and being arrested for public drunkenness—though he never spent more than an isolated night or two in jail. He could pull it all together long enough to cut great tunes like "Ring of Fire" and "Understand Your Man," number-one hits on the country charts in 1963 and 1964, respectively. But by 1965 he had been kicked off the *Grand Ole Opry* show for good, and he even managed to burn down 506 acres (202.4ha) of a California wildlife preserve by dropping a cigarette butt out his car window, for which the government sued him for $82,000. (They collected, too.)

In 1965 Johnny was arrested at the El Paso International Airport by government agents who nabbed him coming back from Mexico. He was smuggling in more than a thousand pills in his guitar—Dexedrine to go up, Equanil to come down: about a two-week supply for Johnny at the time. "One was too many and a thousand wasn't enough," he later admitted in an interview. He was fined and given a suspended sentence—not exactly three years on the chain gang, as his legend has it. In fact, the only two nights he ever spent in jail were in 1965, and one was for the capital offense of picking flowers on private property while drunk in Starkville, Mississippi. (Some outlaw!)

His wife said "enough" and divorced him in 1966, but he started to get at least intermittently straight with the help of singer June Carter, who had cowritten "Ring of Fire." She devoted herself to him,

Opposite: The young Johnny Cash, circa 1957. Above: Johnny with June Carter and their son, circa 1977. Johnny spent most of the seventies absent from the top of the C&W charts, although "One Piece at a Time" hit number one in 1976.

and collaborated with Cash on hits like "Jackson," for which they won a Grammy. The two were married in March 1968, and Cash rose like a phoenix from the ashes of his nearly wasted career. His *Live at Folsom Prison* album, with the new rendition of "Folsom Prison Blues," brought him back to the top of the charts—although his identification with the prisoners on the recording was a little presumptuous for a guy whose "hard time" consisted of a few overnight stints.

"Daddy Sang Bass," sung with June Carter and the Statler Brothers and written by Carl Perkins, was number one for six weeks in 1969, and he had an even bigger hit that summer with "A Boy Named Sue," a novelty tune from an album recorded live at San Quentin; the song hit number two on the pop chart, the biggest of Cash's forty-eight crossover hits, and won him a Grammy. Cash further repaired his credibility by teaming with Bob Dylan for "Girl of the North Country" on the *Nashville Skyline* album, and they performed the song on Cash's television show; Cash also won a Grammy for *Nashville*'s album liner notes.

It was at about this time that Johnny rediscovered his Fundamentalist faith. He studied with Billy Graham for the ministry, a pose he long had fancied. He even traveled to the Holy Land to make a film, *The Gospel Road*, which saw a limited release in 1973; Johnny starred in the film with June Carter, but this tale of the life of Jesus was as stiff as a beanpole. Forgoing his dreams of having his own ministry, Johnny adopted the lessons of his 1971 hit "Man in Black" and swore to always dress in black to signal his identification with the downtrodden (other reasons were cited as convenience dictated). Thus, his 1975 autobiography was predictably titled *Man in Black*.

Johnny spent most of the seventies absent from the top of the C&W charts, although he did reach number one with the clever "One Piece at a Time" in 1976. "I got lazy about recording," he later told *Billboard*. "I was working on a TV show, movies and a book. That's a mistake a lot of artists my age make. But a man only has so much creative energy." He regained some credibility with "There Ain't No Good Chain Gang," a duet with old roommate Waylon Jennings that hit big in 1978. He was inducted into the Country Hall of Fame in 1980. But he also suffered periodic relapses with pills and other drugs, nearly died from a bleeding

Johnny in the midsixties, when his heroic intake of pills cost him his marriage and nearly his career. But with the help of June Carter, whom he later married, Johnny made it back to the top.

ulcer, and even spent time in the hospital with five broken ribs from a wild ostrich attack. (No, we're not making this up.) Forty-four days in the Betty Ford Center for drug rehabilitation in 1983 seemed to have cured him once and for all.

But when Columbia didn't renew his contract in 1986 after twenty-eight years together, Cash was humiliated. Country music stars young and old rushed to his defense in a touching display of loyalty, excoriating Columbia's Nashville boss, Rick Blackburn. But the label had stuck by Cash through many long, dry spells, and business is business. Doubly disappointing was the cool reception of Cash's novel about Saint Paul, *Man in White*, which took more than ten years to write.

Johnny signed with Polygram in 1987, although he publicly expressed dissatisfaction with the job they did promoting him, and the five albums he made for

Rosanne Cash, Johnny's talented daughter, has carved out her own flourishing career, thanks to number-one hits like "My Baby Thinks He's a Train."

them sold poorly. But he now has aligned himself with hipster producer Rick Rubin's American Recordings, for which the first release was the acoustic *American Recordings*. His stark performances of "Why Me, Lord," "Bury Me Not on the Lone Prairie," and "Delia's Gone" earned him his best reviews since the sixties. He also performed with U2 on their *Zooropa* album on "I Went Out Walking," a song the band had written in his honor. Not bad for a grandfather (yes, Rosanne Cash is his daughter) no matter what color togs he sports.

George Jones
TRAPPED IN A HONKY-TONK PRISON

When it comes to behavior, there's bad, there's outrageous, and then there's off the chart. Somewhere beyond even that lies the tale of George Jones, the singer of scores of country classics, the bard behind more than a hundred albums. If there was a Hall of Fame of Self-Destruction, George Jones would be enshrined therein in the most honored spot. He should have been found dead a dozen times by now, but somehow he has eluded the tragic fates that cut short the careers of Hank Williams, Sr., and so many others. Not that he's mean like, say, Jerry Lee Lewis. As one of his former managers remarked, "When George is straight, there's not a more kindhearted person in the world. There's just a little problem with his problems." And those problems nearly buried him in a white blizzard.

Born in Saratoga, a small eastern Texas town, in 1931, Jones was already earning a living as a singer before he could shave. His father was a frequent drunk who George later said made him and his sister play for him long into the night. George dropped out of school in the seventh grade and began playing

George Jones, circa 1967.

guitar for a duo called Eddie & Pearl. After a couple of years in the marines, George found work as a deejay at a Beaumont, Texas, radio station. In 1953 he cut his first record, which helped him get a gig on the *Houston Jamboree* radio show. Late in 1955 he had his first hit with "Why, Baby, Why?" Jones (who had also recorded under the names "Hank Smith" and "Thumper Jones") became a regular on the *Louisiana Hayride* program and in 1959 made it to the top of the country charts for the first time with "White Lightning."

"Tender Years" (1961) and "She Thinks I Still Care" (1962) also hit number one, with the latter earning Record of the Year honors by the CMA. But somehow his momentum had dissipated, and he disappeared into the limbo of the perpetual road show, touching down occasionally for an appearance on *Grand Ole Opry* and making the odd hit here and there ("Walk Through This World with Me" hit number one in 1966). Then he met Tammy Wynette, and everything changed.

The details of their romance, which culminated with their marriage in February 1969, are related on page 39. But it would be remiss not to mention that their performances as a duo (including the Top Ten hits "Take Me" and "The Ceremony") helped reenergize his career. Unfortunately, George's career wasn't the only thing that now shifted into high. Always a heavy drinker, he began training for the Olympic competition in the Jack Daniels event. There is the famous story of George riding his power lawn mower ten (or fifteen, or twenty) miles (16, or 24, or 32km) to a bar after Tammy hid the car keys so he couldn't get drunk. Then there was the time he went AWOL for ten days on a toot; that stunt earned him a packet of divorce papers.

But George charmed his way back, and the couple's duet about the reconciliation, "We're Gonna Hold On," hit number one in October 1973. Nevertheless, Tammy and George were officially divorced a year later. Now George's decline began in earnest. Although he continued to amass Top Ten hits, his concert appearances became increasingly erratic. Sometimes he'd be late, sometimes he wouldn't show at all, and all too often he'd show up in no condition to perform. ("No Show Jones," recorded with Merle Haggard, documented the phenomenon.)

Then George added cocaine to his daily regimen. The Bolivian Marching Powder not only made his last ounce of reliability evaporate, but ate into his finances at an alarming rate. He claimed later that it was his

then-manager, Shug Baggott, Jr., who'd gotten him hooked on cocaine: "Shug got me started on it to keep me messed up, just the way he got me drunk all the time....He robbed me blind." Jones had cause to be perturbed, as Baggott had creatively mismanaged about $2 million in revenues in 1977, and in 1978 George had only $30,000 in assets. In 1979, Baggott was indicted by a federal grand jury for possession and distribution of cocaine and spent a hitch in the pen, but the damage to George Jones—financial and otherwise—had been done. "You name it, and I was doing it," he

once admitted in an interview. "I was about as crazy and messed up as you could get." (And you could get pretty crazy on $2 million worth of cocaine.)

There had been a warrant out for George's arrest because of $36,000 he owed Tammy in alimony, as well as lawsuits from concert promoters ($30,000 for defaulting), furniture stores (over $13,000 in past due bills), banks ($100,000 in overdue loans), and home-owners (for defaulting on a $75,000 purchase). But the most serious charge leveled against him was attempted murder. One September night in 1978, George aimed his .38 pistol at his best friend, Peanut Montgomery, who had recently found God and gone on the wagon. "See if your God can save you now," Jones gloated—and pulled the trigger. Luckily, he was too stoned to aim properly, but he was arrested in Florence, Alabama; eventually, Peanut dropped the charges.

In December 1978, Jones filed for bankruptcy, claiming he was $1 million in debt. In a sour mood, he then beat up his girlfriend, Linda Welborn, who had him arrested for assault and battery. She, too, eventually dropped the charges. But the kindness of friends couldn't keep George from teetering on the precipice; he was doing so much cocaine that his weight had dropped under one hundred pounds (45kg), his gums were chronically bleeding, and he looked like a living skeleton. "I just didn't care anymore," he later explained. The circuits finally blew during a December 1979 concert at the Nashville club Exit/In, for which

Tammy Wynette and George Jones perform on NBC-TV's Nashville Palace *in 1982, during one of their final attempts to reunite professionally; on the personal front, their divorce had long since been finalized. As much as they loved each other, George's addictive personality (first he was on alcohol, then cocaine, then both together) made their 1969 marriage a ticking time bomb that eventually exploded in spectacular fashion. Nonetheless, both Tammy and George are still performing and making artistically successful recordings today.*

he showed up—notable in itself—except that it was not George Jones who performed that night. He sang all his songs in the unmistakable patois of...Donald Duck. Yes, each and every one. Jones was carried off the stage and delivered in short order to Hillcrest Hospital's psychiatric ward in Birmingham, Alabama, the $10,000 cost of which was ponied up by ten fellow performers.

A month later, in January 1980, Jones was released. He announced that he was clean and sober, and

George with his wife, the former Nancy Sepulvada, who more or less saved his life by helping him get straight when most of Nashville considered him a goner. The two were married in 1983.

began mounting an impressive comeback. His new song, "He Stopped Loving Her Today," hit number one, won a Grammy, and was named Single of the Year by the CMA and the ACM; both organizations also named him Male Vocalist of the Year. That year he reteamed with Tammy (whose own career had also seen better days) for an album that yielded the hit "Two-Story House." But what may have saved his life was his winning the love of Nancy Sepulvada, a Louisiana divorcée (complete with children) who had the interest and the patience to try to keep George clean. It would prove to be no small task; George was arrested twice during this time on charges of possessing chemical substances. Within one memorable twenty-four-hour span in 1982, he was arrested by Mississippi police for having cocaine in his car, totaled the car in a crack-up he was lucky to walk away from, and was arrested for drunken driving.

It was around that time that George showed up late for a concert in San Antonio, announcing to the crowd, "I'm drunk, but I love y'all." Half the crowd walked out in disgust. Despite such well-publicized setbacks, he gradually weaned himself from the booze and other inebriants. And Nashville always seemed willing to forgive him one more time; after all, George had mostly been guilty of harming himself. Despite those tumbles off the wagon, he married Nancy in 1983 and moved to Louisiana to live with her—away from the temptations of the big city—hoping he would finally be able to stay clean. And for the most part, he has. In 1992, George was inducted into the Country Hall of Fame, and the ACM also elected him for its Pioneer Award. Both were nice gestures, but what they really should have given the singer was the "Longest Shot to Survive to the Nineties" prize.

Johnny Paycheck

BOUNCED AGAIN

For a guy who's only 5'5" (162.5cm), Johnny Paycheck has been in more trouble than an entire squad of rhino-size fraternity boys. And we're not talkin' panty raids here. This is whippin'-out-the-pistol, pointin'-it-at-someone's-head, then-pullin'-the-trigger kind of trouble. That's the kind that gets you sent to prison, which is precisely where Johnny Paycheck has spent too much of his time. But then, where else would a guy end up who once told a reporter, "Cocaine and alcohol are okay, upfront drugs"?

Born Donald Eugene Lytle in Greenfield, Ohio, in 1938, he learned to play the guitar at six and was strumming it in local talent shows at the tender age of nine. At thirteen he was playing clubs for money—a pro before he had to shave—mesmerizing the customers, who couldn't believe such a big voice was coming out of such a whippersnapper.

The boy grew into a man, but he never grew to a man's height. Young Donald Lytle was fated to remain the size of a thirteen-year-old forever, a bit of genetic fate that led to more than a few brawls with those foolish enough to taunt him about it. He left Ohio and scuffled through the Southwest for a year or so before joining the navy at seventeen.

Some men flourish in the discipline of the military, but for hotheaded Donald it was a match made in hell. One day in 1956 he went AWOL, was dragged back to face charges, and beat an officer nearly to death in the process. That earned him a courtmartial and an eighteen-year sentence for attempted murder; ultimately, the sentence was reduced to two years in the Portsmouth, New Hampshire, military prison. When he was released, it was 1958.

Bidding farewell to the navy, Donald took on the name of Don Young, packed his guitar, and headed for Nashville. There he found work as a backup musician with Porter Wagoner's band. A year later, he shifted to Faron Young's band, and in 1960 he moved again to join Ray Price's Cherokee Cowboys. The restless young Don hooked up with George Jones in 1962, and he stayed a Jones Boy for four whole years. It was during this time that he took the Johnny Paycheck moniker (after a boxer he admired) for his own recordings, which started off as rockabilly but by 1965 had assumed the butt-kickin' sound with which he would thereafter be identified. He had some minor hits, but his big break came when Billy Sherrill bought his song "Apartment #9" for Tammy Wynette to record for her debut. But Johnny let booze—and selected other drugs—derail his momentum. A 1968 arrest for burglarizing a Nashville home made him persona non grata in his adopted town. His punishment was merely a $50 fine, but he knew it was time to move on.

Paycheck split for the West Coast, where he grew increasingly unstable and, as the months went by, became a virtual derelict. "I was living in L.A. just bumming off the streets, working clubs for beer, drinkin' and shootin' up a storm," he later told a reporter. "Right into the frigging gutter." Teetering on the edge, he might have gone over had Billy Sherrill not tracked him down in 1970. Sherrill and one of Johnny's old friends helped him dry out and kick the drugs, got him a gig in a Denver club so he could get his chops back, and eventually took him to Nashville. Sherrill gave him a tune to record that he thought had Paycheck's name all over it, and indeed "Don't Take Her, She's All I Got" became a Top Ten hit on the country charts in 1971. He even felt stable enough to get married. But being Johnny, things didn't run smoothly for long: he bounced a $100 check at a motel and was given a year in jail (the sentence was later suspended).

But his recording career failed to ignite, and by 1976 Paycheck filed for bankruptcy. Again he was on the edge of disaster, and again Sherrill pulled him back. David Allan Coe, another ex-con, had written a song

called "Take This Job and Shove It," and Sherrill felt that felt Paycheck could put it over the top. And in January 1978, he did. The song became his only number-one hit and helped the eponymously titled album go gold, earning him a Grammy nomination and propelling him into the upper reaches of Nashville superstardom. (The darned song was even developed into a half-decent movie in 1981 with Robert Hays, Barbara Hershey, and Art Carney.)

Johnny handled his new success with his trademark perspicacity, spending as much as he could on drugs, alcohol, and the good life. There was a series of nasty lawsuits and countersuits between him and his agent, Glenn Ferguson. Then he was sued for $175,000 by a stewardess to whom he became abusive on a flight from Denver to Casper, Wyoming ("Tell that bitch I have my seatbelt on!"). That very night he dallied with a Casper woman who had attended his concert; unbeknownst to her, he also managed to sleep with her twelve-year-old daughter the same evening. That stunt earned him a statutory rape charge, which would have cost him up to ten years in prison. But he plea-bargained down to a sexual-assault misdemeanor, for which he was fined $1,000 and given a year's probation. (The woman also slapped him with a $3 million civil suit, which was settled out of court.)

Paycheck's money problems only got worse. First, the Internal Revenue Service hit Johnny with a claim for back taxes that totaled over $100,000; the state of Tennessee admired that concept and also came after him; and he had to cough up $26,000 for a 1979 concert he had failed to appear at—all of which forced him to file for bankruptcy a second time. Naturally, his record label, Epic, then chose to let him go, after more than twelve years. "They can take their shit and keep it," he said by way of farewell to Nashville and the music biz. "I've never kissed an ass or licked a boot, and I won't live by their rules."

Johnny PayCheck (formerly Johnny Paycheck) has done his part for charity, from performing to raise money for the Myasthenia Gravis Foundation (opposite) to appearing at this 1986 antidrug rally (above).

Out of work, Paycheck spent most of 1984 and 1985 drinking and doing cocaine, priming himself for the fateful evening of December 19, 1985, at the North High Lounge Barroom in Hillsboro, Ohio. Engaged in a heated argument over the respective merits of turtle and deer meat with a couple of locals who he thought were putting him on, Johnny told them, "I'm gonna mess you up." One of the men, Larry Wise, responded by throwing a punch at Johnny, who whipped out his .22 pistol and shot Wise. Luckily for both parties, the bullet only grazed Wise's head, and he recovered. But the attack earned Paycheck a nine-and-a-half year jail term for aggravated assault with a deadly weapon. ("I was a victim of circumstances," he complained. "It was an accident.") His appeals delayed matters for a while, but what jury could possibly believe that a guy who recorded an album called *Armed and Dangerous* was

just aiming at the ceiling? In 1989 Paycheck was finally sent to Ohio's Chillicothe Correctional Institute to serve out his sentence.

He did just that for two years, acting as a model prisoner and even throwing a concert with Merle Haggard for his fellow inmates. Convinced that Paycheck had really turned over a new leaf, the governor of Ohio, Richard Celeste, commuted his sentence and set him free on the condition that he perform two hundred hours of community service. That was in 1991, and PayCheck—as he now spells his name—has been as good as his word, speaking to schoolkids about the evils of drugs and performing once more at his former level of excellence. Maybe the short singer with the even shorter fuse has truly seen the light, after just thirty-five years or so of raising total hell. And then again, maybe not.

WILLIE
NELSON

WAYLON
JENNINGS

KRIS
KRISTOFFERSON

Ladies
Love
Outlaws

Willie Nelson

NO MORE CRYIN'
IN THE RAIN

You'd have thought he was Al Capone, the way the Internal Revenue Service pounced on Willie Nelson back in 1984 for nonpayment of taxes. His tax shelters had sprung a leak, and Willie—arguably the biggest star in all of musicdom at the time, let alone country music—was on the hook for $16.7 million. Depending on how you look at it, it was either a horrible pickle or an amazing testament to just how far a poor boy from Abbott, Texas, could go. Born on April 19, 1933, at the height of the Depression, Willie was abandoned by his mother when he was only six months old, and his father, an itinerant laborer, wasn't around enough to raise him, either. He went to live with his grandparents, who luckily for him were both musically inclined, enabling Willie to get an early start on the career that would catapult him to stardom.

But first there was the little matter of growing up to attend to. He learned to pick cotton for $1.50 a day, and at night he listened to the *Grand Ole Opry*, like every other aspiring country star. His musical skills helped him escape the day-to-day drudgery when the John Raycheck polka band hired him to play guitar for the astounding sum of $8 to $10 a night—not bad for a kid moonlighting from his sixth-grade studies. He graduated to playing for his brother-in-law's swing band, Bud Fletcher and the Texans, for which his sister, Bobbie, played the piano. After high school he joined the air force, but that stint ended quickly when his bad back gave out.

So he did what any other eighteen-year-old at loose ends would do: he got married. In 1951, he wed Martha Jewel Matthews, a sixteen-year-old waitress who happened to be a full-blooded Cherokee. She kept waitressing while Willie played at night, sometimes in the bar where she worked, while he "daylighted" by selling Bibles door-to-door. Like most teenage marriages, the relationship was stormy more often than not, and there was never enough money and always too many kids—Lana, Susie, and Billy. But somehow the couple kept things going in between some of the world's worst fights, like the time Martha chased a stark-naked Willie through a graveyard while she brandished a knife. Their most famous spat, legend has it, was when a passed-out, drunken Willie was hog-tied inside a sheet and beaten with a broom.

That marriage eventually fought itself out in 1962, and a year later, Willie married Shirley Coolie.

By now he was enjoying some modest fame as a song-writer—he'd written hits like "Crazy" for Patsy Cline and "Hello Walls" for Faron Young—but those successes were mitigated by the alcohol and amphetamines Willie and Shirley were consuming in prodigious quantities. "We were swallowing enough pills to choke even Johnny Cash," he later admitted. Touring regularly, though still not making much money, Willie had an affair with a lovely lady who'd attended one of his shows and stayed on for a private performance, a factory worker named Connie Kepke. Shirley found out about Connie when she opened the mail one day in 1969 and out dropped a bill from the local obstetrician for the baby Connie had just delivered—Willie's, of course. In the best tradition of Jerry Lee Lewis and Myra Gale Brown, Willie and Connie were married in 1971, about five months before his divorce to Shirley finally went through.

That same year the newlyweds moved to Austin, Texas, a counterculture hotbed (compared to Nashville, anyway), where Willie felt free to grow his trademark braided hair and beard and write music that wasn't standard C&W. He cut some albums for Atlantic that were semisuccessful, but when the company closed down its C&W operation, it dropped him. When he moved to Columbia Records in 1974, his masterpiece was already inside his head, just waiting to be laid down on vinyl. *Red-Headed Stranger* was released in 1975 to the sort of universal acclaim that was usually reserved for projects like *Rubber Soul* and *Let It Bleed*—but then, like those unified works of genius, this concept album was much more than just an assemblage of randomly recorded songs. The mystical saga of a preacher in the Old West, *Red-Headed Stranger* was so unique that at first Columbia didn't know what to do with it.

"They thought it was underproduced, too sparse," Willie later told *Billboard*. "They didn't like it, but they

had already paid me for it so they had to release it and they had to promote it." With "Blue Eyes Crying in the Rain" (Willie's choice for the LP's single, over Columbia's protests) hitting number one on the C&W charts, crossing over to the pop charts, and winning a Grammy in the process, the album sold in the millions. A new superstar was born. Smelling gold, Willie cleaned up his act as much as he was able, cutting back on the hard liquor and forgoing drugs entirely—except for his beloved marijuana. Willie once told reporters, "The biggest killer on the planet is stress, and I still think the best medicine [for it] is and always has been cannabis."

Opposite: Willie Nelson, circa 1965, long before he began sporting his trademark beard and braid. *Above:* On the road again: Willie performed more than a thousand concerts from 1984 to 1993 in an effort to pay the Internal Revenue Service nearly $17 million in back taxes.

He and longtime honcho Waylon Jennings self-consciously inaugurated the outlaw movement in C&W by recording the album *Wanted! The Outlaws*, a compilation that features duets between Willie and Waylon, as well as Waylon and his wife, Jessi Colter ("Suspicious Minds," another hit single), and solos by

Willie Nelson and Amy Irving in a passionate moment from the 1980 film Honeysuckle Rose. *Although Amy was married to Steven Spielberg at the time, she and Willie conducted an affair during the making of the movie that reportedly was every bit as torrid as the one they played out on-screen.*

those three and Tompall Glaser as well. The record was named Album of the Year by the CMA, which also named the cut "Good-Hearted Woman" Single of the Year. But more important, *Wanted* became the first country album to go double-platinum, that is, to sell more than two million copies. Waylon and Willie teamed again in 1978 for the number-one anthem "Mamas, Don't Let Your Babies Grow Up to Be Cowboys," which won them a Grammy for Best Duet. But even that smash hit was overshadowed by Willie's next artistic breakthrough, *Stardust*, an album of pop standards. Recording *Stardust* was a bold move, and Willie's renditions of "Blue Skies," "Stardust," and "Georgia on My Mind" (another Grammy winner) gave the songs new life and, just as significantly, broadened Willie's audience by leaps and bounds. (The album eventually sold some four million copies, going double-double-platinum.) Both the CMA and ACM named him Entertainer of the Year in 1979, although Willie was no longer "just" a C&W star.

Hollywood now beckoned, and rather surprisingly, Willie proved himself more than worthy of its interest. He had been unable to realize his dream of having *Red-Headed Stranger* developed into a movie, which was how he had always envisioned its story being told, but he earned a small role in Sydney Pollack's 1979 film *The Electric Horseman*, which became something special when Willie sang "My Heroes Have Always Been Cowboys" as he and star Robert Redford sat around their Las Vegas hotel room. Recognizing Willie's enormous talents, Pollack cannily produced *Honeysuckle Rose*, a

Willie and the Carter Family—Jimmy and Roslyn, that is—convene at the 1980 Democratic Convention, after Willie sang the national anthem. No wonder his tax troubles took place during the Reagan administration!

film designed to showcase Willie dramatically as well as musically, something that had never been done before for a C&W singer—not for Johnny Cash, nor Loretta Lynn, nor Merle Haggard.

Honeysuckle Rose wasn't to be just an extended music video trying to cash in on his popularity. Willie gives a strong performance as Buck Bonham, a C&W star (what else?) whose relationship with his longtime wife, played by Dyan Cannon, is jeopardized when he beds down the young daughter (Amy Irving) of band member and pal Slim Pickens. (Reportedly, Amy and Willie weren't just acting for the camera during their love scenes, which didn't endear either of them to Irving's then-husband, Steven Spielberg.) The soundtrack—which went platinum—featured "Angel Flying Too Close to the Ground" and "On the Road Again," the latter written by Willie on a few minutes' notice at

the request of Pollack during a plane ride. "On the Road Again" perfectly captured Willie's mixed feelings about the road: "After every tour, I swear it'll be my last," he told *Billboard* in 1979, "but after I'm home for a couple of days I'm ready to go back." (His character's chronic infidelity in *Rose* was another subject with which Willie had more than a nodding acquaintance.)

Willie was bigger now than he'd ever dreamed he'd be, big enough to be invited by incumbent president Jimmy Carter to sing the national anthem at the 1980 Democratic National Convention (and, yes, Willie *did* forget some of the words). Another album of standards, *Somewhere Over the Rainbow*, went platinum that same year, and Willie capped off 1980 by being named an "Honorary Convict" by the inmates at the Missouri State Penitentiary, for whom he'd performed a free concert. After savoring the platinum sales of his album *Willie Nelson's Greatest Hits (And Some That Will Be)*, he returned to the big screen in 1982 with *Barbarosa*, a period western in which Willie starred, fittingly, as a legendary outlaw who teaches willing pupil Gary Busey how to survive a life on the run. The film didn't make much of a splash, but Willie's *Always on My Mind* album did, going platinum (so what else is new?), with the single becoming his biggest crossover pop hit.

As the money continued to flow in, he and Waylon combined forces and recorded *Waylon & Willie* in 1978. Then Willie trumped that effort by going on a veritable duet orgy. He and Leon Russell had already teamed for an album called *One for the Road* in 1979, which yielded their number-one remake of "Heartbreak Hotel." Then Willie recorded *The Winning Hand* with Dolly Parton, Brenda Lee, and Kris Kristofferson, then collaborated with Merle Haggard (*Pancho and Lefty*, which Epic mysteriously left on the shelf for a year before releasing it in 1983, at which point the title song became a number-one hit), Ray Price (*San Antonio Rose*), and Faron Young (*Funny How Time Slips Away*). They all went gold, or better.

But those efforts were just business as usual compared to Willie's 1984 collaboration with Julio Iglesias, then the world's best-selling singing star. Julio's ripe ballad style seemed to have as much to do with Willie's deceptively casual, colloquial approach as sangria did with Jack Daniels. But after hearing him on the radio, Willie decided that he and Julio were fated to record together, and their song "To All the Girls I've Loved Before" was another chart-topping crossover smash. In

The Highwaymen —from left to right: Willie Nelson, Waylon Jennings, Johnny Cash, and Kris Kristofferson—gear up for a 1985 performance. During this time, Willie was also performing solo in the Farm Aid concerts, recording duets with everyone from Leon Russell to Ray Charles to Julio Iglesias, acting in films, and selling hot dogs at Yankees games.

1985, Willie and Ray Charles had a number-one hit with "Seven Spanish Angels." Also in 1985, he made *Highwayman*, the title song from which won a Grammy, with Kris Kristofferson and Johnny Cash.

But suddenly Willie's platinum touch struck a thorn. The Internal Revenue Service, taking stock of all those millions and millions of record sales, toasted Willie for his success with a $6.5 million judgment in 1984 for nonpayment of taxes and another $10.2 mil-

lion in penalties and interest—a whopping $16.7 million in all. The IRS seized most of Willie's property and other assets, and he had to sell, auction, and hock almost everything else that wasn't tied down. "I've been calling around looking for one of those suicide machines," he told *Rolling Stone*, tongue firmly in cheek. "I'll go on national TV, hook myself up to that machine and tell everyone I have 'til 7:00 to get $16 million. If I don't, I'm pulling the plug."

Now Willie was an outlaw for real, and he found it wasn't much fun. (Perhaps it's not surprising that Willie, the architect of the Farm Aid concerts, which existed because of the U.S. government's indifference to the plight of farmers, would become the apple of the IRS' unforgiving eye.) For the next several years Willie worked for the government, performing two hundred nights a year and recording albums like the wittily titled *Who'll Buy My Memories? (The IRS Tapes)*, a collection of his early acoustic music, to whittle down that debt. A million here, a million there, and the debt still loomed in front of him, as big as the Sierra Madres. To add insult to injury, the movie version of *Red-Headed Stranger* (completed in 1984), with Willie as the reincarnated preacher and Morgan Fairchild and Katharine Ross as the women in his life, was finally released in 1986 to the sound of a deafening thud.

Plenty of new gold albums would follow, *The Troublemaker, Take It to the Limit, Half Nelson, Willie & Family Live*, and *Willie Nelson Sings Kristofferson* among them, but that dark cloud of debt was still over

his head. He gained a small (tiny, really) measure of revenge with his scathing political protest song "Living in the Promiseland," which hit number one in 1986. After the publication of his autobiography, *Willie*, in 1988, he recorded *A Horse Called Music*, which brought him another number-one song, "Nothing I Can Do About It Now"; actually, the song didn't refer to his tax troubles, although the philosophical attitude of the title did express Willie's state of mind. "I've been broke before and I will be again," he remarked in an interview with *The New York Times*. "Heart-broke? That's serious. Lose a few bucks? That's not." (The "few bucks" finally amounted to $9 million, the figure Willie and the IRS settled on in 1993.)

And so Willie forges on, making more movies, remarrying in 1991 (Connie filed for divorce in 1987), and having two children with his fourth wife, Ann Marie D'Angelo. But the suicide of his thirty-three-year-old alcoholic son, Billy, on Christmas Eve in 1991, left Willie devastated. Willie threw himself back into his work, mounting the Farm Aid V concert (following the ones from 1985, 1986, 1987, and 1990, which collectively raised tens of millions of dollars for beleaguered farmers) and trying to start up the Outlaw Music Channel/Cowboy Television Network. His newest album, *Moonlight Becomes You*, is another collection of standards ("Sentimental Journey," "You Always Hurt the One You Love") with two original tunes by Willie snuck in; released in 1994, it demonstrates that his interpretive powers are still top notch.

But old habits die hard: in May 1994 Willie was arrested by police in Hewitt, Texas, who found him sleeping on Route I-35 in the backseat of his Mercedes, with two ounces (56.7g) of pot. He was handed a misdemeanor drug charge—"a part of life," Willie commented—then released on $500 bond, just in time to record his version of "My Way" for Frank Sinatra's second *Duets* album.

Willie with his third wife, Connie Kepke, and their children, circa 1980. Willie and Connie were married from 1971 to 1987.

Waylon Jennings

THIS OUTLAW BIT'S DONE GOT OUT OF HAND

He was the yang to Willie Nelson's yin, a rootin'-tootin' hard-ass whose tootin' got him into a big peck o' trouble. Clad in black leather with a cigarette hanging out of his mouth, James Dean style, Waylon Jennings was half of the outlaw movement that revolutionized country music in the midseventies. He could walk that walk and talk that talk like few others—when he wasn't so messed up on pills and powder that he'd trip over his own cowboy boots and slur his words, that is.

Born in Littlefield, Texas, on June 15, 1937, Waylon grew up on country music but started grooving on rock 'n' roll when it caught fire in 1956. A Lubbock, Texas, deejay named Hipockets Duncan took a shine to Waylon and hired him to spin discs at KLLL, a country station, while he performed on the side. When

Buddy Holly, whom Hipockets had discovered a few years back, stopped by KLLL to visit his old mentor, Waylon was introduced to Holly and the two hit it off. Holly helped Waylon record some songs, acting as his producer and even inviting Waylon to move to New York and live with him and his wife, Maria. "He was the first man that ever had faith in me as a singer," Waylon later recalled. When Holly split from the Crickets late in 1958, he hired Waylon to play bass for his new backup band, knowing that Waylon had never before played the instrument. Waylon was given a week and a half to learn it, and he accepted the challenge.

The Winter Dance Party, as the tour was named, headlined Holly but also featured such acts as Dion and the Belmonts, the Big Bopper (J.P. Richardson), and Ritchie Valens. They opened in Milwaukee on January 23, 1959, then cut across the Midwest, traveling by bus to half the cities in Wisconsin, Minnesota, and Iowa. Their promoter filled in a free date with a gig in Clear Lake, Iowa, and Holly—sick of life on the tour bus—chartered a plane for himself and his band to fly on ahead. But the Bopper, who had a cold, begged Waylon to give up his seat and switch to the bus so that he could recuperate. Waylon agreed, a generous act that saved his life. For that was the plane that never made it, crashing shortly after takeoff and killing Holly, the Big Bopper, and Valens (who had also traded off with a band member at the last minute, flipping a coin for the seat).

"Everything just seemed a waste after Buddy died," Waylon reflected. Traumatized by the loss of a friend and also by guilt, he gave up his dreams of a musical career for several years and returned to being a deejay. In 1963 he moved to Phoenix and began playing in clubs again, building enough of a local reputation to earn a recording contract with RCA after Bobby Bare saw him perform in 1965. Waylon agreed to move

to Nashville, where he roomed with Johnny Cash, and Chet Atkins began producing his music. Some minor hits (and major hangovers) followed, and Waylon even won a Grammy for his 1969 cover of "MacArthur Park." But his career wasn't progressing the way Waylon wanted it to; he felt constrained playing by Nashville's rules. He did cut "Ladies Love Outlaws" in 1972, an infectious tune that might have become the anthem for the outlaw movement had it not been a few years ahead of its time.

Then he and old drinking buddy Willie Nelson decided to cut loose and shake up the town. They began performing together, making music that melded elements of rock, folk, and Texas-style country, delivered in a loud, roughneck, take-no-prisoners, expect-no-bullshit manner. It was like a blood transfusion for Waylon, who scored his first number-one hit, "This Time," in 1974; the *This Time* album was coproduced by Waylon and Willie, and signaled Waylon's new direction. His follow-up singles, "I'm a Ramblin' Man" and "Rainy Day Woman," also hit the top of the C&W chart. But it was the defiant "Are You Sure Hank Done It This Way?"—his 1975 indictment of the Nashville establishment—that threw down the gauntlet for Waylon. Both it and the B side, "Bob Wills Is Still the King," made it onto Waylon's first number-one album, *Dreaming My Dreams*.

"Good-Hearted Woman" was ostensibly a live performance by Willie and Waylon, who had written the song together in 1969. But Waylon, who'd recorded it solo in 1972, actually put it together himself in the studio. "Willie wasn't within ten thousand miles when I recorded it," he boasted, and it hit number one in 1976 all the same. So did the album it ended up on, *Wanted! The Outlaws* (see page 70 for details). With that album, Waylon hadn't simply arrived—he'd taken the whole damn fort.

But what would a great success story be if the hero didn't screw up big-time at some point? Waylon had always exhibited a bit of a chemical-dependency problem, chomping down amphetamines at such a rate back when he was rooming with Johnny Cash that he later admitted, "It got to the point where it nearly killed both of us; I weighed 135 pounds [60.75kg] soaking wet." But that was before he was in the limelight, and he sure *looked* healthy enough. From 1972 on, Waylon had been building a whopper of a cocaine habit, which became the source of his downfall in

One of the most successful recording duos of all time, Willie Nelson and Waylon Jennings redefined the limits of country music by defying all of Nashville's outmoded conventions.

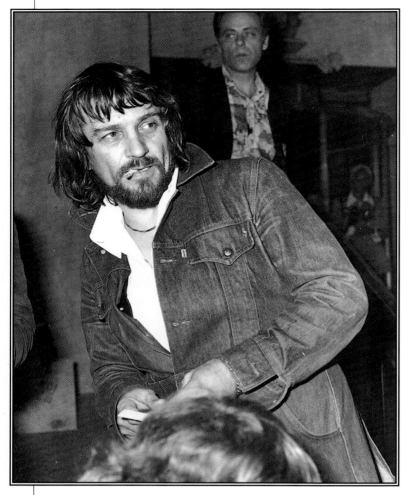

Waylon *attends a 1976 charity dinner for "Actors and Others for Animals" at the Beverly Wilshire Hotel.*

1977. He had just been savoring back-to-back number-one hits, with the single "Luckenbach, Texas (Back to the Basics of Life)" and the album *Ol' Waylon* (which would soon go platinum) when, on August 24, he was arrested for possession of twenty-seven grams of cocaine. But the way the events occurred was more the stuff of a Marx Brothers farce than high tragedy.

A courier package addressed to Waylon and marked "Confidential: Do Not Open" was in fact opened by the New York messenger, who found the twenty-seven grams therein. He told his boss, who alerted the FBI, who let two grams go through to their destination—a Nashville recording studio—in preparation for a nice, clean bust. They got the bust all right, but luckily for Waylon the narcotics agents were too stupid to observe the basic legalities (they never caught

Waylon with the cocaine, as he had flushed it down the toilet before they came in), ensuring that the fifteen-year sentence Waylon was given in court was overturned. (For fans of irony—and who isn't one?— Waylon had been named an honorary police chief by the Nashville police a few months before.) He commemorated the event by recording "Don't You Think This Outlaw Bit's Done Got Out of Hand?"

Not that Waylon, who had been putting about $1,500 a day in powder up his nose, had learned any kind of lesson from that close call. He was sued in 1978 for destroying a motel in Flagstaff, Arizona, after a concert. High as a kite, he trashed not just his room, like a good ol' rock star would have done, but most of the building. He was playing with fire, but it didn't seem to affect his record sales. "Mamas, Don't Let Your Babies Grow Up to Be Cowboys," a duet with Willie Nelson, hit number one early in 1978 and won a Grammy, and their album *Waylon & Willie* went double-platinum. "I've Always Been Crazy," a song he admits he recorded while coked to the gills, went to the top later that year, and his ballads "Amanda" and "Come With Me" reached number one in 1979. In 1980 he had number-one hits with a pair of outlaw anthems: "I Ain't Livin' Long Like This" and "Good Ol' Boys," the theme from *The Dukes of Hazzard* television series, which Waylon also narrated.

The money was pouring in, but Waylon was stuffing it up his nose with both hands. He wasn't eating, he wasn't sleeping, he could barely perform, and he was practically broke—the owner of his recording studio had sued him for a cool $750,000 for damages and operating costs that had accumulated. Waylon's wife, Jessi, kept him alive by force-feeding him health shakes of her own invention, but he was teetering on the edge. Finally he couldn't even record a song without passing out halfway through it. "I Ain't Livin' Long Like This" began to take on chilling overtones.

A long talk with Johnny Cash, who'd recently managed to kick his pill habit, helped encourage Waylon to go cold turkey. "I can look back now and tell what a wreck I was," Waylon reflected some time later. "I was really, really sick. A lot of folks had tried to tell me that for a long, long time, but I wouldn't listen." He moved to an isolated house in Scottsdale, Arizona, in 1984 with Jessi and their son, Shooter, and gritted his teeth. A month later he was clean. He returned to Nashville, asked his band members to jettison their drugs when working with him henceforth, and dove back into his music.

The project that brought Waylon back to the top of the C&W charts was *Highwayman*, a concept album he cut in 1985 with Willie Nelson, Johnny Cash, and Kris Kristofferson. The record was the year's most exciting country venture, with five of the ten cuts featuring all four artists, and the other five various groupings of them. The title cut, written by Jimmy Webb, won a Grammy for Song of the Year and hit number one, while the album sold a million copies. (A *Highwayman II* album followed in 1989.) Most recently he scored an artistic success with his wonderfully titled album *Too Dumb for New York City, Too Ugly for L.A.*, although it didn't sell like his triumphs from the seventies. But Waylon evinced a glimmer of humor when he commented on the new wave of handsome, hunky country stars who had taken his place in the spotlight: "If me and Willie were starting out now, we'd be in a lot of trouble."

Waylon and his wife, Jessi Colter, often performed together. While she proved to be his "Good-Hearted Woman," he was living up to the self-destructive sentiments of "I Ain't Livin' Long Like This."

Kris Kristofferson

WHY HIM, LORD?

He's probably the only Rhodes scholar to hit it big in country music—hell, half of Nashville's performing stars were trying to clear up the time to study for their high school equivalency diplomas while he was teaching college. But handsome Kris Kristofferson left academia and the military to squeeze himself into several careers at once: Sensitive Songwriter, Movie Star, Outlaw Recording Artist, Multimedia Sex Symbol, and Heavyweight Boozer. He could do it all, and sometimes he did it all at once. Maybe he just squeezed too hard.

Born in Brownsville, Texas, in 1936, Kristofferson was raised an army brat, the son of a two-star general.

He joined ROTC while playing football and boxing in college; he even made the Golden Gloves. Then came the prestigious Rhodes Scholarship to Oxford University, and he joined the dons to study the mystical poetry of William Blake. Trained as a pilot in the army, he rose to the level of captain. But when he was invited to teach English at West Point in 1965, he decided to head to Nashville instead. A prizewinning writer of short stories, he now wanted to write and perform his own songs. But he had to prove himself first, which in Nashville meant bartending and mopping up the Columbia Records studio after hours. With a wife and two kids, a little of that went a long way. Then the wife and kids went as well, and Kris—who at twenty-nine was no kid—was about to give up when Roger Miller (composer of "King of the Road") decided to record his song "Me and Bobby McGee." Now Kris had Nashville's attention.

Kristofferson had written "For the Good Times" while piloting helicopters for offshore oil rigs in the Gulf of Mexico. Ray Price recorded the song, and in 1970 it hit number one, winning a Grammy as well as Song of the Year and Single of the Year awards from the ACM. At the same time, Johnny Cash invited Kris to guest-star on his television show and recorded "Sunday Morning Coming Down" (now *that* must have struck a chord with the Man in Black!), which won the 1970 CMA Song of the Year award.

In 1971, his composition "Help Me Make It Through the Night" won Grammys for both composer Kris and performer Sammi Smith. It also won Smith the CMA Single of the Year award, and went gold for her. Nor did it hurt when Janis Joplin's cover of "Me and Bobby McGee" hit number one posthumously on the pop charts, introducing the Kristofferson name to the rock culture. It was the beginning of his crossover success, but hardly the end. He also launched his acting career by starring in the film *Cisco Pike* with Gene Hackman and Karen Black; he also wrote the score, which included the great tune "Lovin' Her Was Easier (Than Anything I'll Ever Do Again)."

Hotter than a pistol, Kris earned his first gold records with the number-one single "Why Me (Lord)?" and his albums *Jesus Was a Capricorn* and *The Silver-Tongued Devil & I* in 1973. His screen sideline continued to build with a nice part in Paul Mazursky's *Blume in Love* as Susan Anspach's stoned, blissed-out musician boyfriend, and the lead role in Sam Peckinpah's *Pat Garrett and Billy the Kid*. Neither film was a smash, but, still, he was working with two of the day's top directors. One of his costars in *Billy* was the beautiful Rita Coolidge, and be-

fore you knew it the two were an item. They performed together, winning a Grammy in 1973 for their duet "From the Bottom to the Bottle," and were married that August. They won another Grammy for "Lover Please" from their *Full Moon* album, which went gold. To top it off, Kris was getting more film work, including a good supporting role in Martin Scorsese's *Alice Doesn't Live Here Anymore* in 1974. Kris was a long way from West Point and William Blake's poetry. Life was a bowl of cherries.

But if that was the end of the story, Kris Kristofferson wouldn't be in this book, would he? Fame's usual pitfalls stretched before him, and like so many others before and since, he stepped right in and pulled the hole over him. Kris' longtime indulgence in

Opposite: Kris Kristofferson came to Nashville's attention when Roger Miller recorded his song "Me and Bobby McGee." Above: Kris and Rita Coolidge in 1973. They shared a Grammy, a gold album, and wedding bands. But Kris' wandering eye soon created an irreparable rift between the two.

light recreational drugs was one thing, but his heavy drinking—once acceptable in heavily sociable Nashville—escalated into a major problem.

Everything came to a head during the filming of *A Star Is Born* in 1976, his biggest movie to date. Cast opposite superstar Barbra Streisand by producers Streisand and her then-boyfriend, now–Hollywood mogul Jon Peters, Kris played a rock star whose fall from the top led to his inexorable disintegration because of drugs and alcohol. It wasn't much of a stretch. Kris was so out of it on the set that Streisand had to scream at him to get him to play his scenes right, and it's hard to tell if he ever did. When he watched himself on-screen months later, he was so shocked by his dissipation that he swore to give up alcohol then and there, news that delighted Rita. But all he managed to

do was switch over to industrial-strength doses of marijuana, which kept his physical appearance up, if not his ability to form a coherent sentence.

Kris let his musical work go to pot as well, concentrating instead on acting in films like *The Sailor Who Fell from Grace with the Sea* (the *Playboy* photo spread which included a shot of Kris with his head buried deep between costar Sarah Miles' legs; Rita loved that one!), *Semi-Tough* (again in character as a stoned-out football quarterback), *Convoy* (the C.W. McCall hit, via Sam Peckinpah, who, according to Kris, turned him into "a basket case"), *Rollover* (Kris as a rogue investment banker—great casting, guys!), and that disaster of disasters, *Heaven's Gate*. By now his marriage to Rita had ended in divorce, and the film offers understandably slowed to a trickle. "I was pretty

A scene from 1976's remake of A Star is Born, *in which Kris plays John Norman Howard, a charismatic rock idol whose love affair with the bottle soon capsizes his romance with rising songstress Esther Hoffman (Barbra Streisand). Offscreen, life was not much different: Kris' drinking problem was just one of the many conflicts that scuttled his marriage to Rita Coolidge.*

Johnny Cash and Kris Kristofferson in the late eighties. The two have known each other since the midsixties, when Kris used to sweep out Johnny's CBS recording studio in Nashville after hours.

heavy into chemicals," he later admitted in an interview. Kris Kristofferson had fallen off the merry-go-round, but good. "Fame is like being in a public [outhouse], and everybody's writing on the wall," he remarked bitterly of his celebrated difficulties.

Kris got a reprieve in 1984 when he made the movie *Songwriter* with Willie Nelson, a good if little-seen film directed by Alan Rudolph in which Kris plays a C&W singer who has to help old pard Willie out of a jam; the part fits Kris like a glove, and there's some nice music to boot. Kris and Willie teamed again in 1985, joining with Waylon Jennings and Johnny Cash to record one of the year's most successful albums, *Highwayman* (see pages 72 and 79), which helped boost his musical career.

In 1987, Kris recorded an album that was highly critical of Ronald Reagan's policy in Nicaragua, *Repossessed*; even though the record didn't sell well, it helped reestablish his musical credentials. He looked great as a futuristic private detective in the film noir *Trouble in Mind* (1987) opposite Keith Carradine and Genevieve Bujold, and also received good reviews for his work in the television miniseries *Amerika*. He teamed up with Willie and *Payday*'s Rip Torn for *Pair of Aces* in 1990, a made-for-television western with Kris as a modern-day Texas ranger and Willie as a safecracker; it spawned a sequel, *Another Pair of Aces: Three of a Kind*. But even though Kris' life and health seem to be back on track, will Nashville ever forgive him for turning his back on her? His 1994 release, *Singer/Songwriter*, was a double-CD set split half into Kris' own singing, half into covers of his songs by performers like Ray Price and Johnny Cash. The album was an effective reminder of how potent a force Kristofferson was twenty years ago, before he let himself be seduced by the glitz of La-La Land.

They're Gonna Put Me in the Movies

COUNTRY ON THE BIG SCREEN

Sissy's sweet soprano cuts through the coal dust in Coal Miner's Daughter, *the best C&W biopic yet.*

Best Biopic

Coal Miner's Daughter (1980). This version of the life of Loretta Lynn, adapted from her autobiography, won an Academy Award for Sissy Spacek, and is the only movie about a real-life country star ever nominated for Best Picture. Sissy somehow manages to sing Loretta's greatest hits herself, instead of relying on lip-synching as Jessica Lange did in *Sweet Dreams*, the 1985 film in which she played Patsy Cline. Kudos to Tommy Lee Jones as husband Mooney Lynn and Levon Helm as daddy Ted Webb.

Runner-Up: *Your Cheatin' Heart* (1964). George Hamilton, Jr., played Hank Williams; Hank, Jr., supplied his father's songs. But things were done tamely back then—let's make it again with the gloves off! (With Christian Slater?)

Greatest Cameo Performance

Jerry Lee Lewis' blazing rendition of the title tune from *High School Confidential* (1958), performed on the back of a moving flatbed truck over the opening credits.

Runner-Up: Willie Nelson singing "My Heroes Have Always Been Cowboys" in *The Electric Horseman* (1979).

Best Country Song Written for a Movie

Kris Kristofferson's "Lovin' Her Was Easier (Than Anything I'll Ever Do Again)," performed in his film debut, *Cisco Pike* (1972).

Runner-Up: Bob Dylan's "Knockin' on Heaven's Door" from Sam Peckinpah's *Pat Garrett and Billy the Kid* (1973).

Kris Kristofferson (right) strums a few chords for another lost soul in his fine movie debut, Cisco Pike.

Silliest Big-Budget Movie about the Country Music Experience:

Rhinestone (1984). This may also qualify as the Worst Movie of All Time. Dolly, Dolly, Dolly—what *were* you thinking of? (The $3 million, probably.) And Sly Stallone—oy!

Runner-Up: *Urban Cowboy* (1980), if only for the miscasting of John Travolta—although to

Best Movie about the Country Music Experience

Payday (1973). This is a blistering look at the excesses of a performer's life on the road, with a really nasty performance by the great Rip Torn dredging up echoes of the misadventures of Hank Williams, Sr., George Jones, Merle Haggard, and half of Nashville's other bad-boy stars. Still timely after more than twenty years.

First Runner-Up: *Nashville* (1975). Robert Altman's Oscar-nominated film is great and gets points for letting Ronnie Blakely, Keith Carradine, Karen Black, and the other actors write and perform their own tunes (Carradine's "I'm Easy" was that year's Oscar-win-

ning song)—although the metaphoric baggage gets a bit heavy.

Second Runner-Up: *Honeysuckle Rose* (1980). Willie Nelson's star turn is surprisingly convincing, even when he's bedding down young Amy Irving, his best friend's daughter. Good tunes, too, by Willie ("On the Road Again" was nominated for an Oscar), Emmylou Harris, and Johnny Gimble.

Barbara Harris rallies the crowd after a shocking assassination attempt by singing "It Don't Worry Me," in Robert Altman's Oscar-nominated Nashville.

give credit where it is due, he did learn to dance like a son of a gun. Debra Winger is just yummy and Scott Glenn is the meanest villain since Basil Rathbone. But take away the great soundtrack by Mickey Gilley ("Lookin' for Love"), Bonnie Raitt, and the Charlie Daniels Band, and what have you got? An Italian kid from New Jersey who looks real funny in a Stetson.

Best Low-Budget Showcase for C&W Performers

Country Music Holiday (1958) with Ferlin Husky, June Carter, The Jordanaires—and Zsa Zsa Gabor!

Runner-Up: *From Nashville With Music* (1969) has George Jones, Merle Haggard, Buck Owens, and Marty Robbins performing amid a really stupid plot.

Opposite, top: John Travolta in the 1980 box-office smash Urban Cowboy, *a film that yielded one of the biggest-selling soundtracks ever. Opposite, bottom: Zsa Zsa Gabor as the Queen of Country? She was better cast in her other 1958 movie,* Queen of Outer Space. *Above: George Jones, before he became a chronic no-show, performs with his band in 1969's* From Nashville With Music.

Kris Kristofferson played the irrepressible "Rubber Duck" in Convoy, *a 1978 film in which truckers rebel against outmoded speed laws, corrupt police officers, and shady politicians.*

Best Movie Based on a C&W Hit

There's not a whole lot to choose from here, but Sam Peckinpah's *Convoy* (1978) has trucker Kris Kristofferson leading bad cop Ernest Borgnine, a thousand cruisers, and hundreds of giant semis on a cross-country chase across the interstate highways. Dumb, but it does full justice to the 1975 C.W. McCall hit that bears its name.

Most Unnecessary Use of a Song to Base an Entire Movie On

"Middle Age Crazy," a 1977 hit by Jerry Lee Lewis, was turned into an awful movie with Bruce Dern and Ann-Margret in 1980.

Runner-Up: Kenny Rogers' humongous 1978 hit "The Gambler" spawned four made-for-television movies, including *Kenny Rogers as the Gambler* (1980) and *The Luck of the Draw: The Gambler Returns* (1991)—although the latter does get points for providing Reba McEntire with her big-screen debut...tied with *Take This Job and Shove It* (1981), an "opening-up" of the great Johnny Paycheck tune that really didn't require any embellishment (although this isn't really that bad a movie).

Best Impersonation of a C&W Performer by an Actor Who Never Was One

Robert Duvall in *Tender Mercies* (1983), hands down. He won an Oscar, but who'd have thought he could write and perform all of his own songs? Betty Buckley also impresses here.

Most Promising Debut in a Recent Film by a C&W Star

Lyle Lovett as a detective in Robert Altman's *The Player* (1992).

Most Assured Performance by a C&W Star in a Non-Singing Role

Mac Davis as the hotshot quarterback in *North Dallas Forty* (1979), tied with Willie Nelson as the legendary outlaw in *Barbarosa* (1982) and Dolly Parton in *9 to 5* (1980)—although doing the theme song too is kinda cheating.

Best Year for C&W Music in the Movies

A close call, but it looks like 1980 has it, with *Honeysuckle Rose, Coal Miner's Daughter,* and *Urban Cowboy*—how about those soundtracks?—plus *9 to 5,* just for Dolly's debut.

Worst Year for C&W Music in the Movies

1980 again, because of *Middle Age Crazy* and *The Gambler.*

Top right: Robert Duvall gives a great, Oscar-winning performance as Mac Sledge, a surly, inarticulate, but gifted C&W singer-songwriter, in 1983's Tender Mercies. *Above:* Mac Davis (far right) is a cocky pro quarterback (loosely based on former football great Joe Namath), and Nick Nolte (center) is his screwed-up, tight-end pal in the fine adaptation of Peter Gent's novel North Dallas Forty.

GLEN
CAMPBELL

BILLY RAY
CYRUS

GARTH
BROOKS

Rhinestone Cowboys

Glen Campbell
RHINESTONE HUBBY

It's not likely that there has ever been a wider credibility gap between a country music performer's public image and private life than we find with apple-cheeked, sweet-voiced Glen Campbell. Millions grew up watching him perform on *The Smothers Brothers' Comedy Hour* in the late sixties, bantering cheerfully with the Smothers before launching into sensitive tunes like "Wichita Lineman" or the antiwar ballad "Galveston." Who'd have dreamt that within a few years he'd turn into one of the most disloyal, selfish, cruel, misogynist SOBs in the Western Hemisphere?

Born the seventh son and one of twelve children of a preacher-man in Billstown, Arkansas, in 1936,

Glen grew up picking cotton. He would have eaten it if he could have, the family was so poor. Glen dropped out of school at fourteen to join the band of his uncle, Dick Bills, in New Mexico, and played with them for four years. There he met fifteen-year-old Diane Kirk; they were married when Glen was seventeen, after he got her pregnant. (Their premature baby died a few days after birth.) They had another baby, Debby, a year later. But when Glen found that Diane was stepping out on him, he divorced her and moved to Los Angeles. The year was 1958.

In Los Angeles, Glen played wherever and whenever he could, but he struggled constantly. In 1959 he entered a sixteen-year marriage with Billie Jean Nunley, an Albuquerque

beautician he had met while playing that town. Only Billie Jean's ability to find work as a bank cashier kept the couple afloat the first few months of their marriage, but then Glen's gigs improved. He joined the instrumental band the Champs for a spell in 1960, and it wasn't long before he found himself much in demand as a session musician. He backed up Ricky Nelson, eventually going on tour with the erstwhile teen idol. The work paid well, but he knew he was as good as—hell, *better* than—many of the popular singers he was playing behind.

He got his chance to prove his talent in 1961, when he cut his own composition "Turn Around, Look at Me." The song barely cracked the Hot 100 (although several years later the Vogues made it a Top Ten smash). Chastened, Glen began composing and singing advertising jingles—his most famous was the "Is it true blondes have more fun?" ditty for Lady Clairol. His first national exposure came as a backup singer and musician on the television show *Shindig* from 1964 to 1965, and he played at being a rock star after being invited to tour with the Beach Boys as an honorary "Boy" in 1965, having played and sung backup on a number of their records. He even played guitar on "Strangers in the Night," gazing reverently at Sinatra as Ol' Blue Eyes sang. After the session, Sinatra asked his producer who "that fag guitar player was."

Things were starting to break for Glen, and in 1967 they exploded, for that was the year he recorded John Hartford's "Gentle on My Mind," a lovely, perky ballad that practically swept the country music categories for the 1967 Grammys, taking Best C&W Recording, Best C&W Male Solo Performance, Best Male Vocal Performance, and Best C&W Song (this last one went to Hartford as the composer). The ACM also named Glen the top male vocalist, and *Gentle on My Mind* the Best Album and Best Single Record of the Year. But the song's lyrics conveyed a message of male

Opposite: Glen Campbell thanks two young fans for a birthday cake with a little pickin' on the balcony of his hotel on April 23, 1970. Above: Latter-day Glen, with short hair and a beard, shows evidence of years of hard livin' on his brow.

independence and, yes, infidelity that Campbell's current and future wives and lovers would have been wise to pay heed to.

The same could be said of his follow-up smash, "By the Time I Get to Phoenix," a gorgeous Jimmy Webb composition about a roaming soul with a chicken-shit disappearing act (pay attention, ladies!). It, too, crossed over in a big way, going gold and winning Glen Grammys for Album of the Year and Male Vocalist of the Year. The CMA in 1968 cited him in numerous categories as well, including Song of the Year

Glen with Sarah Barg—now his former wife and former wife of former good friend, Mac Davis—in 1977.

("Wichita Lineman," another Jimmy Webb creation), Album of the Year (*Glen Campbell and Bobbie Gentry*), Male Vocalist, and Television Personality (he had hosted the summer replacement show for the Smothers Brothers and actually topped their ratings). Life was sweet, and Campbell was an enormous star—not just in country, mind you: in 1968 he actually outsold the Beatles!

Success breeds success, and Glen made the leap to the next level of fame by appearing in two movies, first as John Wayne's insufferably self-righteous sidekick in the 1969 hit *True Grit*, then as the freewheelin' ex-marine buddy of Joe Namath in the 1970 flop *Norwood*. Even though Glen's record sales had cooled down and his CBS-TV series *The Glen Campbell Goodtime Hour* had ended its three-year run in 1972, he was still bigger than most country stars had ever dreamed of being. When "Rhinestone Cowboy" hit number one in August 1975—it would go on to be named the year's top-selling country single—he was back on top.

By this time success was finally going to Glen's head. Along with the requisite carousing common to stars of a certain magnitude, Glen had been going behind the back of golfing buddy Mac Davis, whose wife, twenty-two-year-old Sarah Barg, Glen lusted after. In September 1975, Billie Jean filed for divorce from Glen; in October, Sarah filed for divorce from Mac, for reasons he didn't comprehend at the time. But Mac got the picture a week later at the Country Music Awards, which he and Glen were cohosting; as Glen was handing out awards, someone broke the news to Mac backstage that Sarah and Glen were living together. "I'm not making excuses for what I did," the born-again Glen says of the situation in his autobiography, *Rhinestone Cowboy*. "My judgment and values were distorted because of the alcohol and cocaine."

As soon as the divorce proceedings were finalized (cost to Glen: $2 million), Glen married Sarah, telling the press that he still considered Mac his friend. (No doubt Mac felt the same way.) The couple rented a house in Beverly Hills for $6,000 a month and proceeded to party. "Sarah and I centered our life around cocaine," he now admits. "Sometimes we did it day and night, at home or on the road." But in 1980, three weeks after she had given birth to their son, Dillon, Sarah left Glen, claiming he had been unfaithful to her. (Some shock!) All he had to show for their drug-addled relationship was a bunch of gold records (including CMA awards for Song of the Year and Record of the Year for "Rhinestone Cowboy") and a $3 million settlement to Sarah.

But that marriage wasn't the only one made of rhinestones. In fact, it was just a warm-up for the Glen Campbell–Tanya Tucker World Series of Romance. Tanya and Glen had met in 1973 backstage at the Country Music Awards, when she was fourteen and he was thirty-six. But Tanya was a precocious kid; born

Young Tanya Tucker dreamt of laying in a field of stone—little knowing just how rocky her love life with Glen Campbell would soon be.

in Seminole, Texas, the same year that Campbell was getting married for the second time, she'd had a hit with "Delta Dawn" (blowing Helen Reddy's original off the map) when she was just thirteen. By the time she was a high school freshman, she'd hit number one with "What's Your Mama's Name?" and "Would You Lay with Me (in a Field of Stone)?" (She kissed school goodbye then and there.) Admitting she'd had a crush on Glen for years, she called him approximately ten minutes after he separated from Sarah, and before the ink on the divorce papers was dry, Tanya and Glen were an item. When they made the cover of *People*

A somewhat addled Glen and Tanya croon sweet nothings on stage. An hour later they were probably clobbering each other with hotel furniture! The relationship ended with a $3 million lawsuit, months in rehabilitation, and lots of bitter memories.

magazine, the tagline read: THE WILDEST LOVE AFFAIR IN SHOWBIZ TODAY. He was forty-four and a grandfather with five kids; she was twenty-one. Campbell gushed, "Tanya is my first love. Golf is my second."

The love affair was a good career move for both of them. They cut hit songs together, made a television special, and even sang the national anthem in 1980 at the Republican National Convention. Glen gave Tanya an engagement ring before the year ended, with the wedding scheduled for Valentine's Day, 1982. But the relationship was not to be. The insecure Campbell began to grow increasingly paranoid about Tucker's devotion to him—without cause, as it turned out, but then those skintight, black leather outfits of hers weren't designed to make her look like a housefrau.

"Dating Tanya to escape cocaine was like jumping into a lake to avoid getting wet," Glen says of her in his relentlessly self-serving autobiography, *Rhinestone Cowboy*. "How warped I was back then." (A bit later in the book, he describes how he almost died while freebasing, something Tanya wasn't stupid enough to try.) He eventually dropped her from his British tour and withdrew funding from her Beverly Hills boutique, the Rhinestone Cowgirl. Their affair had lasted just fifteen months, but it took Tanya years to recover, both personally and professionally. Her acute cocaine addiction finally landed her at the Betty Ford Center in 1988. "I respect her efforts to recover, but have wondered if they worked," Glen gallantly comments in his book. "I'm inclined to pray for the woman with whom I shared a poisoned relationship."

"I was a carnal Christian," he confesses. But he wiped the powder off his nose long enough to somehow woo and marry wife number four, Kimberly Woollen, a former Radio City Music Hall dancer, in 1982. (They remain married today, and have had three children together.) As a belated wedding present,

Tanya slapped him with a $3 million lawsuit in 1985, charging him with assault and battery, mayhem, and fraud. The case was settled out of court.

But Tanya got the last laugh. In 1986 she had her first number-one song in more than ten years, a rebirth she celebrated by having two children out of wedlock with television actor Ben Reed (the couple remain unmarried but claim to be raising the children together). Tanya cemented her career comeback by being named Female Vocalist of the Year in 1991 by the CMA and having her 1992 album *What Do I Do with Me?* go platinum. Invited to perform at halftime at the 1994 Super Bowl, she lip-synched, strutted, and writhed in a tight black outfit that could only be rated "R."

As for Mr. "God wanted me to tell the truth": his music career seems stuck in first gear. It's been forever since one of his songs topped the charts, as he now concentrates on what he describes as "contemporary Christian hits." (His latest album is his latest claim to innocence, *The Boy in Me*.) Most of the year he performs at the Grand Palace in Branson, Missouri—not exactly the Great White Way, but then, there are less sinners out there. And he's still golfing, often with Alice Cooper, who now teaches Sunday school. Never mistaken for a rocket scientist, Glen continues to espouse his beliefs on the respective roles of men (Lord of the Mansion, master of all he surveys) and women (chattel that can cook). But why not let Kim have the last word: "Glen, today, is flesh-and-blood proof that God can change a life. Glen once just lived, but today he is alive!" Now, if he'd just shut up.

Top left: The mature, confident, Glen-less Tanya today, whose own reborn career has gone to outshine born-again Glen's (above) by a wide margin.

Garth Brooks

LOVIN' THAT "CHASE" TOO MUCH

Country music has always had its share of groupies, and if it hadn't, Hank Williams would have had to invent them. But when country and western recently started selling as only rock 'n' roll used to, the stakes were upped dramatically—and not just in dollars. Bigger paydays were part of the scene, to be sure, but so was more glamorous exposure and more far-reaching fame. All of which guaranteed that country's biggest stars were fated to encounter groupies in far greater numbers—and with much greater persistence—than those who had haunted the Opry in the heyday of Red Foley and Roy Acuff. It was all part of the new, glitzier territory.

Garth Brooks, country's biggest star in the nineties, learned that lesson, up-close-and-personal. Named 1993's top recording artist by *Billboard*—not just for country, but all of musicdom—Brooks came up the old-fashioned way: he earned his fame by touring 200 to 250 days (and nights) of the year. When you're on the road that much, temptation looms large, and opportunity knocks often. By the time his first album, *Garth Brooks*, yielded a number-one single, "If Tomorrow Never Comes," and brought him to national attention in 1989, Garth Brooks was a trophy that any self-respecting groupie would have given her eyeteeth to notch on her garter belt. As Brooks now admits, an awful lot of them did. Unfortunately, Brooks was a married man who really wasn't free to dally. And his wife made that abundantly clear when word of his peccadilloes reached her ears.

Born in Yukon, Oklahoma, on February 7, 1962, Troyal Garth Brooks (wonder what happened to that "Troyal"?) had a mother who, as Colleen Carroll, had recorded a few singles for Capitol in 1955. Her music never caught on, and she gave up her career to raise her family, Garth and his five older brothers and sisters. With his mother as inspiration, along with the banjo she bought him when he was six, Brooks was soon consumed by country music. When he was a little older, he taught himself the guitar and decided to be a professional singer when he grew up. He was awarded a track scholarship to Oklahoma State University, graduating in 1984 with a degree in advertising. Garth then headed to Nashville with his guitar and a demo tape. Two days later he was back in Oklahoma at his parents' house, rejection ringing in his ears, wondering what it would take to break into the music business.

What it took was the usual years of paying dues. Garth worked as a bouncer in bars, where he also got the chance to perform, often before just a handful of bored patrons. But he honed his skills and waited for the break that would make Nashville pay attention. While he was waiting, he married his college girlfriend, Sandy Mahl, and took a job in a Nashville boot store, where many famous feet presumably walked in and asked to be shod. He also wrote songs for other performers, as well as ditties for Lone Star Beer and other companies to use in their commercials. An audition with Capitol finally led to a recording contract in 1988—his advance: $10,000—and with the backing of a major label, his touring began in earnest.

But as he performed with his band, Stillwater, before ever more enthusiastic crowds all over the South, Garth noticed that some of his female fans began asking for autographs without bothering to ex-

tend a piece of paper. What Sandy, who often accompanied him, thought as she watched him signing one heaving bosom after another can only be imagined, but Brooks did tell *People* magazine that she once threw an overly friendly fan off the stage ass-over-teakettle. The trouble was, she wasn't always there to play chaperone, and Garth began to take advantage of the free samples that were being waved under his nose. "I just dove in and had a blast," he admits ruefully. Pretty soon Garth was sampling the whole darn candy store.

Not surprisingly, word of his extracurricular activities trickled down to Sandy, who confronted him. At first he stonewalled her, denying everything. But then

Garth signing autographs for fans at the City of Hope Ball Games in Nashville, June 1993.

conscience struck. "I poured my guts out to the woman, told her I'd lied," he recalls. Sandy put him on trial, and he pledged to turn over a new leaf, even apologizing to her during an interview with Barbara Walters on national television. "I didn't deserve a second chance, but I got one," he now marvels.

On his second album, the million-selling *No Fences* (1990), Garth included a song called "The Thunder Rolls," in which the perils of adultery are limned with dramatic results. In fact, in the video for "Thunder," Garth himself played the unfaithful, wife-battering husband who gets his just deserts when his wife shoots him dead. "I enjoyed being the asshole," he explained, "because [the video] showed that the asshole doesn't win." *No Fences* was named the Album of the Year by the ACM, which also selected his

Garth—with his wife, Sandy, and without his trademark hat—at the Country Music Awards in 1993.

"Friends in Low Places" as Single of the Year and "The Dance" as Video of the Year. In 1991, he won a Grammy for "Ropin' the Wind." He was named Entertainer of the Year by both the ACM and the CMA in 1991 and 1992. And when *Forbes* magazine did a story on the big business of country music, who do you think they used as their cover boy?

He now spends most of his free time with his daughter, Taylor (after folksinger James) Mayne Pearl Brooks, and his newborn baby, rarely leaving his estate in Goodlettsville, Tennessee, except to tour. And when he does tour, which is frequently, Sandy and the kids usually accompany him. But if Garth's sportin' life has come to an end, it certainly hasn't affected his creativity or popularity. His 1992 and 1994 television specials were showy and iconoclastic, churning up acres of both praise and vilification for his willingness to cross country's ancient boundaries of "good taste." His pro–gay rights stand, clarified in his song "We Shall Be Free," has left much of Nashville perplexed, if not downright miffed.

All the hullabaloo still puzzles Brooks a bit. "There's better songwriters and singers than me," he recently mused. "Lots of better-looking guys, too. And I can't pick a guitar hardly at all." Yet he must be doing something right, because *The Chase*, his third album, shipped quintuple-platinum (sold five million units) and broke in at number one on the pop charts, the first country album ever to do so. *The Chase* just may end up being the biggest-selling country album of all time. (That ought to beat signing your name on some beautiful stranger's chest any day of the week.)

What the future holds for Garth is unclear, but his reign seems likely to continue for some time—even if his fourth album, *In Pieces*, didn't make the initial megasplash of *Fences* and *Chase*. But with a newly svelte torso (no more "Pillsbury Doughboy" jokes!) and a wildly successful European tour under his belt, his

Garth in 1994—slimmed down and made-up.

biggest problem would seem to be keeping track of the awesome achievements he can claim for his first five years in the biz: sixteen number-one singles; $35 million in album sales; ten ACM awards; nine CMA awards; four People's Choice Awards; and (rather surprisingly) just a lone Grammy. But none of that has gone to Garth's head. As he told *Playboy* in a 1994 interview, "Did you ever think that the largest-selling artist of the nineties would be going bald and have an eating problem?"

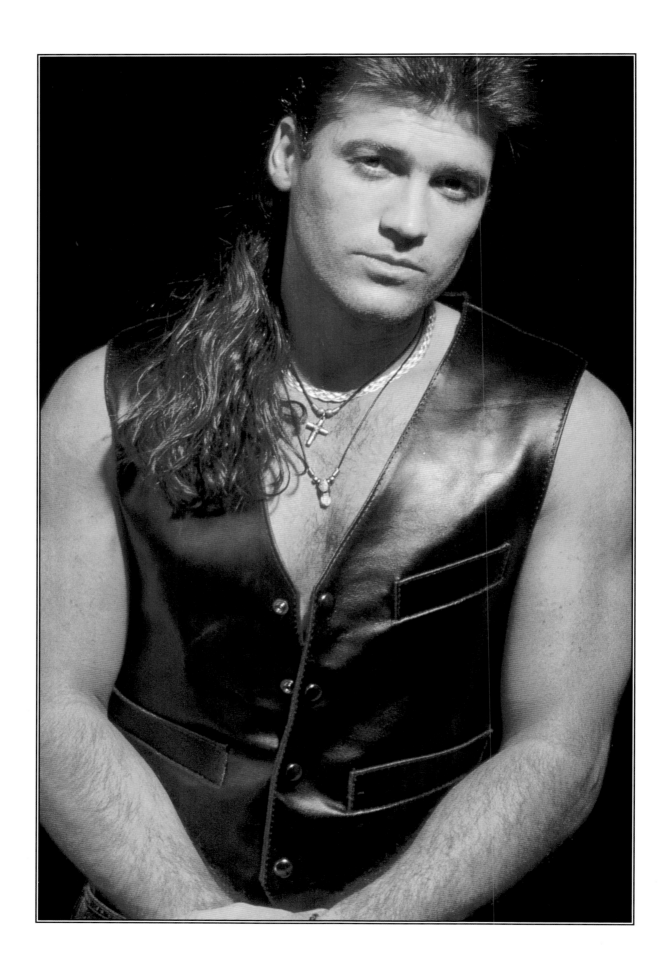

Billy Ray Cyrus

ARE YOU SURE HANK DONE IT THIS WAY?

"I don't consider myself a hunk," Billy Ray Cyrus once confessed in a fit of modesty. But that's like the Incredible Hulk saying he doesn't consider himself to be green. What's there is there, and those millions of women aren't screaming at Billy Ray because they've been touched by his sensitive lyrics. No, it's that buffed body, displayed in all its sweaty glory bursting out of a wee bit of a sleeveless shirt, that inspires a feeding frenzy whenever he performs—like dribbling some bloody chum into the water to attract the trailing sharks. In short, Billy Ray Cyrus is the first rhinestone cowboy who has been able to bypass the actual rhinestones while achieving his desired effect: desire.

Billy Ray was born in Flatwoods, Kentucky, on August 25, 1961—a year after Merle Haggard was released from prison, but a couple of months ahead of the birth of k.d. lang. Patsy Cline and Jimmy Dean were riding high on the C&W charts with "I Fall to Pieces" and "Big, Bad John," and Billy Ray's dad was performing with his gospel group, the Crownsmen Quartet. When he was just four, Billy Ray was already getting up in church to accompany the Crownsmen on "Swing Low, Sweet Chariot" as his mother played the piano, his grandmother the organ, and his dad the fiddle. But—hard as it is to imagine now—he was a nerdy kid whose clumsiness and shyness kept him from even dancing at school parties.

He dreamed of playing baseball, so to compensate for his physical deficiencies, Billy Ray began doing five hundred push-ups a day and pumping iron. Never

were calisthenics and metal put to better use. He bulked up enough to make the high school team as a catcher, and then the baseball team at Kentucky's Georgetown College. But when he realized that he never would be good enough to play professional ball, he laid down his mitt and picked up a guitar. The muscles he was stuck with.

First, he had to teach himself to play the guitar, which he did while assembling his first band, Sly Dog. In 1982 the band began playing bars and clubs in Ohio

Opposite: Billy Ray Cyrus, the hunk of country, was once so shy and awkward that he didn't dance at school parties. Above: Billy Ray putting his baseball skills to use at the City of Hope Ball Games in Nashville, 1993.

and Kentucky, gradually building a local reputation as a band with real kick. But the demos Billy Ray had been sending to Nashville were ignored, and in 1984 he packed up and moved west, hoping he could make his break in the Los Angeles music scene. Something broke, all right, but it was Billy Ray's spirit; after three years of selling cars to support his dream of a performing career, he admitted defeat and moved back to Flatwood. "I had to get back to my roots," was his explanation, and his hunch was correct, for a few days after he arrived, he met his wife-to-be, Cindy Smith.

Billy Ray also hooked up with his old pals from Sly Dog, and soon the band was back in business, playing year-round at the Tagtime Lounge in Huntington, West Virginia. Nearly every Monday Billy Ray would make the twelve-hour round-trip drive to Nashville, bearing his latest stack of demos. His efforts finally paid off in 1988, when veteran singer Del Reeves recorded one of Billy Ray's tunes and signed him to a contract. Before long, he was opening for Reba McEntire, which in turn gave him the exposure to get a recording deal with Mercury. His first album consisted mostly of songs

Billy Ray posing with his wax likeness at the Movieland Wax Museum, Buena Park, California, June 1993.

A one-shot wonder? Billy Ray maintains that he's here to stay. Another thirty years of hits and he'll almost have caught up with George Jones.

came Billy Ray's anthem, a bouncy showcase for his neo-Elvis gyrations that quickly attracted a fanatical female following. One especially dedicated group of ladies (so to speak) called themselves the Cheerleaders, and when it came to Billy Ray they weren't taking any prisoners: one of them set Cindy Cyrus' hair on fire with a cigarette lighter, a conflagration doused in a timely manner by a bystander with a handy pitcher of beer.

Shortly thereafter, Cindy threw Billy Ray out and initiated divorce proceedings. Billy Ray was so busy you'd think he wouldn't even notice—but he did, penning a heartfelt tune called "Where'm I Gonna Live" to commemorate the night Cindy tossed his stuff out on the lawn. When the song became a hit, he gave Cindy half the royalties and a coauthor credit. (Now *that's* sensitive!) In October 1991 the divorce became final. Looking back on the experience of being married to him, Cindy insists, "We're really better friends now than ever." For his part, Billy Ray mused, "I don't think true love ever goes away....I just hope when she looks back on Billy Ray Cyrus, she'll be able to say I was a good-hearted man—but *just* a man. Just a dude."

Billy Ray Cyrus was now fair game. Just in time, too; the maddeningly catchy "Achy, Breaky" was released on April 6, 1992, to a slavering mob and fueled by the constant play of the video with a sweaty Mr. Cyrus giving all. The song went gold instantly. His album *Some Gave All* followed a month later, hitting number one on the pop charts in its second week, and ultimately going quintuple-platinum in the United States and selling another ten million copies around the rest of the world, making it by far the biggest

he wrote or cowrote, but there was one ditty penned by another hand that Billy Ray decided to add at the last minute.

Originally called "Aching, Breaking Heart" when Don Von Tress submitted it around Nashville, the song had been rejected so many times that Von Tress could hardly complain when Billy Ray converted the title to "Achy, Breaky Heart" after the audiences he'd been playing it to began calling it that. "Achy" quickly be-

debut album in music history. His follow-up single, "Could've Been Me," also hit number one (although it's practically the answer to a trivia question at this juncture). Billy Ray–mania ruled.

But the bigger the money, the more plentiful the litigation. The Cyrus Virus brought everyone out of the woodwork who'd so much as had a cup of coffee with him in the old days. Both Del Reeves and his wife, Ellen, sued Cyrus for royalties and percentages of gross

earnings they claimed were due them for their early support. More seriously, at least two paternity suits surfaced shortly after his star went into orbit. The first was filed by Kristen Luckey, a South Carolina waitress with whom Billy Ray had had a fling shortly after his divorce. He acknowledged that little Christopher Cody Cyrus was his, and immediately began paying child support. "I love this baby son," he enthused. Another suit was filed by a Kentucky woman who'd appeared in the "Achy, Breaky" video; again, Billy Ray said he'd pony up if the child proved to be his. "I wouldn't be the first man to have two babies," he accurately observed. (But he might be the first to have two millionaire babies.)

Those kinds of problems, and his classy handling of them, earned points for Billy Ray. And he needed them, because his October 1992 induction into the Country Hall of Fame inaugurated a tidal wave of jeers. After all, the guy had had exactly one hit single and one hit album up to that point—so wasn't this honor just a bit premature? Not at all, huffed Irving Waugh, the elderly producer of the CMA awards show, pointing out how much Billy Ray had done for the industry even in so short a time. But that didn't stop Waylon Jennings and Travis Tritt (to name but two peers) from criticizing him as a flash in the pan—the rhinestone syndrome, as it were. Nor could it keep parodies like "Achy, Breaky Butt" from flooding the airwaves. Of course, any semblance of privacy in his life went up in smoke long ago.

Billy Ray with his daughter, the optimistically named Destiny Hope, at the Pyramid Arena in Memphis, Tennessee, in October 1994. They were attending "Elvis, the Tribute."

But then, he'd had all the privacy he wanted and more for most of his life, and it hadn't satisfied him. With the success (in sales, if not reviews) of his 1993 follow-up album, *It Won't Be the Last*, ensuring that he isn't just a one-shot wonder, Billy Ray has been able to temporize about being the much-dissed sex symbol to millions: "Even with all the bad things, I'm a lucky man." A lucky, ducky dude, indeed.

Country's Most Persistent Myths

1) Hank Williams, Sr., died of heart failure, as his death certificate attests.

2) Dolly Parton had breast augmentation surgery early in her career.

3) Spade Cooley (above, in the film *Casa Mañana*) stomped his wife to death as their teenage daughter, Melody, watched.

4) Loretta Lynn is psychic.

5) Merle Haggard, Johnny Cash, Waylon Jennings, and Johnny Paycheck have all served time in a penitentiary.

6) Glen Campbell used to pass out in his bathtub so frequently that his wife had to check regularly to make certain he hadn't drowned.

7) Burt Reynolds nearly drowned in Tammy Wynette's bathtub.

8) Preacher Jimmy Swaggart, singer Mickey Gilley, and all-purpose wildman Jerry Lee Lewis are all related.

9) Jerry Lee Lewis married his fourteen-year-old cousin, Myra Gale Brown.

A N S W E R S

1) False; he probably asphyxiated on his own vomit after passing out from massive doses of vodka, tequila, morphine, and chloral hydrate pills. All medical workups done on his corpse—per order of his mother, Lilly—quickly vanished, so the more respectable "heart attack" explanation can never be refuted for certain. 2) False; she's the truth! 3) Unfortunately, this is true; it happened on April 4, 1961. 4) True; at least according to some folks who've had their palms read by her. (So why didn't *she* predict Billy Ray Cyrus?) 5) False; Cash and Jennings never suffered more than an overnight lockup, and not so many of those. 6) True; you couldn't make this stuff up. 7) True (as revealed in Tammy's autobiography *Stand by Your Man*). 8) True; they are all first cousins and second cousins. See Nick Tosches' great biography *Hellfire: The Jerry Lee Lewis Story* for the full, mind-bending explanation. 9) False; Myra Gale was thirteen when she wed Jerry on December 12, 1957, although the marriage certificate lists her age as twenty.

JIM
REEVES

JOHNNY
HORTON

BARBARA
MANDRELL

PATSY
CLINE

CARL
PERKINS

The Endless Sleep— and Some Near Misses

Whenever a beloved performer meets a gruesome fate, it's stop-the-presses time at newspapers and magazines all over the world. Rock 'n' roll has enjoyed (to use the word loosely) the most spectacular tragedies, ranging from Buddy Holly's 1959 plane crash to the corpse of Elvis slumped next to his Graceland toilet (or one of his toilets, to be precise) in 1977 to Kurt Cobain killing himself with a gunshot wound to his left temple in April 1994. The untimely passing of a movie star probably engenders the biggest headlines, with the deaths of James Dean (car crash, 1955) and Marilyn Monroe (who knows?, 1962) still the all-time shockers. More recently, there was the drug-overdose death of River Phoenix monopolizing front pages and editorial columns worldwide.

But when a country star meets an unexpected end—or just barely survives meeting one—there's something distinctively, well, country about it. Some of those sudden passings, like that of Hank Williams, Sr., are covered elsewhere in this volume. What follows is a survey of the events that changed the shape of C&W music, sometimes temporarily, often permanently, and inevitably for the worse.

Johnny Horton

He had one of the biggest hits of the decade with the number-one crossover smash "Battle of New Orleans," winner of two 1959 Grammys. "Sink the Bismarck" and "North to Alaska" were also million-sellers, back when that number actually meant something. Not so long before, Johnny Horton had been earning his living as a fisherman. In fact, it was while performing as "The Singing Fisherman" that Johnny had first made an impact on the Louisiana television shows *Home Town Jamboree* and *Louisiana Hayride* in the midfifties.

Johnny had been married since September 1953 to Billie Jean Williams, who nine months earlier had been widowed by Hank, Sr., and was living with her and their two children in Shreveport when he traveled to Austin to perform at the Skyline Club on November 4, 1960. After the performance, Johnny, guitarist Herald Tomlinson, and manager Tillman Franks decided not to stay the night, but instead to go back to Shreveport in Horton's sweet white Cadillac. Shortly after one in the morning they were struck by a 1958 Ford driven by a very drunk nineteen-year-old Texas

Opposite: The day the music died: the Iowa cornfield where Buddy Holly, Ritchie Valens, and the Big Bopper met their maker after their plane crashed in February 1959. Above: Johnny Horton's premature death in a 1960 car crash robbed country music of one of its biggest crossover successes.

A&M student. Johnny, who was driving, was killed instantly; his friends survived, as did the student. Johnny Cash delivered the eulogy at Horton's funeral.

But Billie Jean, to whom fate had dealt a cruel blow again, saw to it that a number of Johnny's home-recorded vocals were produced with studio musicians and released by Columbia over the next several years, thus keeping alive the legacy of her second husband.

Patsy Cline

The greatest female country singer of her generation, Patsy Cline almost met her maker two years before the 1963 plane crash that ultimately took her life. Already riding high on the charts with what would prove to be country's number-one song that year, "I Fall to Pieces," Patsy was involved in a head-on car collision on her way to a grocery store in Madison, Tennessee, in June 1961. A woman in the other car (whose fault the accident was) died instantly; Patsy was hospitalized with broken ribs, a dislocated hip, and a number of lacerations. She spent a month in the hospital and additional time recuperating in a wheelchair, and for quite a while those broken ribs kept her from reaching her high notes. But in less time than seemed possible, Patsy was hobbling out onto the Opry's stage, crutches and all, to sing her soaring songs. (One member of the audience was a young Dolly Parton, who raved about the performance.)

Patsy recovered fully and found that she was more popular than ever. More big hits followed, like "Crazy" (written by Willie Nelson) and "She's Got You." On Sunday, March 3, 1963, she played a benefit

Patsy Cline nearly died in a 1961 head-on auto crash and spent more than a year painfully recovering from the accident to reach the point where she could perform again. But her efforts seemed all for naught when her plane went down on a rainy night in Tennessee in March 1963.

concert in Kansas City for the family of deejay "Cactus Jack" McCall, who'd been killed in a car accident. Cowboy Copas and Hawkshaw Hawkins, who were also on the bill, decided to fly back to Nashville with Patsy in her single-engine Piper Comanche plane that Tuesday. The plane was piloted by her manager, Randy Hughes, who made the first half of the run successfully. But when he landed in Dyersburg, Tennessee, to refuel, Hughes was told that heavy rain and strong winds lay ahead, and was advised to lay over in Dyersburg until the weather had abated. For whatever reason, Hughes decided not to wait and called ahead to his wife to tell her he'd be home in three hours.

The plane never made it to Nashville. A search party was sent out that night, but it wasn't until the morning of March 6 that a farmer, W.J. Hollingworth, found the wreckage scattered over an oak-tree-

covered hill in Fatty Bottom. None of the bodies, which on impact had been thrown hundreds of feet from the plane, was still in one piece. Patsy Cline was thirty when she died. (A morbid postscript to the story is that, on his way to her memorial service, *Opry* performer Jack Anglin of Johnny and Jack was killed when his car ran off the road and crashed into a tree.)

Although she was gone, Patsy continued to have hit records, beginning with the single "Sweet Dreams," which was released a week after her death. But at least one of her albums from the hereafter was in less than good taste: in 1981 some genius electronically faked Patsy singing posthumous duets with Jim Reeves, who had died in 1964. The 1985 film about her life, *Sweet Dreams*, was okay (Jessica Lange didn't even try to sing Patsy's songs herself—probably a sensible idea, come to think of it), but paled in comparison to the 1980 biopic about Loretta Lynn, *Coal Miner's Daughter*, starring a singing Sissy Spacek.

Jim Reeves

"Mr. Velvet" was what some of Nashville called him, but it wasn't really meant as a compliment. Jim Reeves was the other end of the spectrum from Jerry Lee Lewis and his ilk, a soft-spoken smoothie who planed off his rough Texas edges after making a name for himself on *Louisiana Hayride* in the early fifties (his big break: Hank Williams was a no-show one night and Jim filled in). To some, Reeves' songs seemed more than a bit saccharine—"Four Walls," "He'll Have to Go," "A Touch of Velvet"—but they and dozens of others were big, big hits, the epitome (to some minds) of C&W class, with nary a twang to be heard nor a bottle of beer to be swigged amid the strings and polite confessions of heartbreak.

Touring an average of three hundred days a year, including highly successful jaunts across Europe and

Jim Reeves died in 1964, a year after Patsy Cline's fatal plane crash. Nonetheless, Jim and Patsy "recorded" an album in 1981, thanks to the wonders of modern studio technology.

South Africa, Reeves had learned how to pilot a plane, the better to take himself from one concert to the next and also keep abreast of his vast real estate holdings. On July 31, 1964, he and piano player Dean Manuel rented a single-engine Beechcraft Debonair and flew to Arkansas to examine a potential property acquisition. They then turned around and began the four-hundred-mile (640km) return trip to Nashville, where Reeves was due to appear on the *Opry* the next night. The pair almost made it, but just twenty miles (32km) away from home a storm kicked up that was severe enough to make Reeves call air traffic control at Beery Field for information. That was the last anyone ever heard from Jim Reeves.

A search party of seven hundred that included such country music luminaries as Stonewall Jackson, Chet Atkins, Eddy Arnold, Marty Robbins, and Ernest Tubb fanned out through the suburb of Brentwood, finally finding the wreckage on Sunday, August 2. The pieces of the Beechcraft were scattered through the woods of Old Baldy. The event was almost a replay of the previous year's Patsy Cline disaster: the bodies were damaged beyond recognition.

While it's common for the sudden death of a beloved performer to spur record sales immediately afterward (Patsy Cline, Elvis, Buddy Holly), Jim Reeves probably holds the postmortem record. He actually had six number-one hits over the next three years—including one in 1965 morbidly titled "Is It Really Over?"—and charted sporadically into the eighties, not to mention that grim album of posthumous "duets" with Patsy Cline.

Carl Perkins

The original king of rockabilly, Carl Perkins, was riding high with his national hit "Blue Suede Shoes" on the morning of March 22, 1956, when he was being driven in a rented limousine to New York City, where appearances on the popular television showcases *The Perry Como Show* and *The Ed Sullivan Show* promised to elevate him into mainstream stardom. Those shows could do for Carl what they'd done only recently for Elvis, who just a couple of months before had enjoyed his first number-one hit with "Heartbreak Hotel."

But the promise of that golden future was derailed—almost permanently—when the limousine struck a stalled pickup truck at about 6:30 A.M. just outside of Dover, Delaware. The driver of the pickup, who'd been sitting in the cab, was killed, and one of Carl's passengers suffered a broken neck. Carl himself was rushed to the hospital with severe spinal injuries

Carl Perkins might have been as big as Elvis Presley if his career hadn't come to a screeching halt after a near-fatal car crash in 1956. Now we'll never know.

and a fractured skull. From his hospital bed, where he spent the next nine months, Carl watched Elvis perform his cover version of "Blue Suede Shoes" on *The Jackie Gleason Show*.

Pretty soon everyone had forgotten about Elvis' 6'6" (2m) challenger, and it wasn't until years later—when the Beatles recorded some of Carl's early songs, such as "Matchbox" and "Everybody's Trying to Be My Baby"—that people realized Carl was still alive. He has since returned to performing on the bar and club circuit, but the glory that might have been his was left on the side of the highway that morning in 1956. On the other hand, he did outlive Elvis after all.

Barbara Mandrell

On September 11, 1984, Barbara Mandrell and her children, Matthew and Jaime, completed their shopping expedition at the Rivergate Mall, got into her silver 1982 Jaguar, and headed home to Hendersonville, Tennessee, on Route 31. On the way, they were struck by a Subaru that crossed the center line and hit them head-on. The Subaru was driven by Mark White, a nineteen-year-old University of Tennessee student who on this particular occasion had neglected to fasten his seatbelt. White never got another chance, either; he was instantly crushed to death. "It was obvious the driver of [that] car was dead," an observer told inquiring reporters. "There was no question in anyone's mind about that."

But Barbara and her children had been wearing their seatbelts, and all were alive when the police arrived on the scene. Barbara was trapped behind the wheel, with half of the dashboard imbedded in her chest. She was rushed to Baptist Hospital in Nashville for emergency surgery. She had a broken leg, a broken ankle, broken ribs, a crushed knee, and a concussion, along with dozens of lacerations on her face. She also suffered (temporarily) from amnesia, and had to have a steel rod inserted in her leg to help her thighbone heal properly. It took her more than six months to recover enough to go out in public.

In 1985, Barbara's fans were gratified when she recorded a new album, *Get to the Heart*, and announced that she and her husband, Ken Dudney, were going to have another baby. But in September she shocked her fans and the rest of Nashville by announcing that she had filed an $8 million lawsuit for negligence against the late Mark White (who had no traces of alcohol or drugs in or on his person). That sum projected her lost earnings due to the crash. A $2 million lawsuit for pain and suffering was also filed, and

smaller amounts were claimed on behalf of her son ($200,000), daughter ($100,000), and husband ($25,000 "for the loss of the services...of his wife"!).

Although Barbara had recently won back-to-back awards as the CMA's Entertainer of the Year—the first woman ever to do so—and had even had her own television variety show on NBC, her popularity could not survive this kind of public-relations blunder. Hate mail was delivered to her door by the bushel basket, and anti-Barbara jokes swept the town. Her record sales plummeted, and although they eventually stabilized, she has not had another number-one hit. Even the 1990 publication of her self-pitying autobiography *Get to the Heart* couldn't entirely restore the luster that she lost when she put a price tag on what seems to have been just a terrible, terrible accident. But she's still a draw on the concert circuit, and has been a spokesperson for the National Safety Council's "Please Buckle Up!" campaign.

Barbara Mandrell suggests we all buckle up: that's good advice that's good for her image, too. But Barbara's petty lawsuit against the estate of the student who died when his car crashed into hers has had quite a negative impact on her image in Nashville.

We Fell to Pieces

(ACCIDENTS AND TRAGEDIES IN BRIEF)

Of course, not *all* of the tragedies involving country stars were disasters that *befell* them; in some cases, the stars themselves were the agents of harm. Here's a short list of some of C&W's darkest moments:

SPADE COOLEY

In the early morning hours of April 4, 1961, Dennel Clyde "Spade" Cooley—one of country's most beloved fiddlers, bosom buddy of Roy Rogers, and sometime movie star—beat his thirty-seven-year-old wife, Ella Mae, to death at their ranch just north of Willow Springs, California. The latter stages of the murder were conducted in view of their fourteen-year-old daughter, Melody, who was told by Spade that her dying, blood-spattered mother had just fallen through the glass doors of their shower. Spade then proceeded to stomp Ella Mae to death with his boots; Melody watched until she ran screaming from the house.

The police were given the same story about the shower accident, with the additional fillip that Ella Mae had also been hurt a few days before when she jumped out of a moving car to account for the cuts and bruises all over her face and body. But the coroner's report noted Ella Mae had a ruptured aorta, cigarette burns on her chest, and lacerations inside her vagina and anus. "I must have hurt her terrible," Spade later testified. "I felt horrible. I was ashamed of her. I was ashamed of myself." His excuse was that she had provoked him by admitting to an affair with Roy Rogers, and that she wanted to join a sex cult. But a neighbor testified that Ella Mae simply wanted to leave Spade. (Can't imagine why.)

During the lengthy trial, Spade fainted twice, and even suffered a heart attack. But the jury found him guilty of first-degree murder anyway, and the judge sentenced him to life imprisonment at Vacaville Prison. Eight years later he dropped dead moments after receiving a standing ovation for his performance (he was periodically allowed out of jail to perform under supervision) at a policeman's benefit concert at the Oakland Coliseum.

Spade Cooley and former girlfriend Anita Aros fiddled the night away in 1953; eight years later, Spade stood trial for the first-degree murder of his wife, Ella Mae.

JERRY LEE LEWIS, who had the brass to tell talk-show host Geraldo Rivera "I've never hit a woman in my life" on camera, despite uncountable cases of his clobbering various wives (and other women) having already come to light. Myra Gale, to name but one, swore in her 1970 divorce plea that Jerry Lee had punched her "black-and-blue" in front of their seven-year-old daughter, Phoebe, when his supper wasn't readied quickly enough for him once in the middle of the night. He also threatened to throw acid in her face if she ever left him. He was sued by a Tennessee woman who claimed he dragged her across a piano during a nightclub performance (but, hey—no extra charge!), and of course there were the two wives who died under *very* mysterious circumstances. Maybe what Jerry Lee meant to tell Geraldo Rivera (see page 22) was what he once boasted in another interview: "I never hit anybody—unless I want to." But then, this was the guy who once shared this thought with an unappreciative audience: "I hope you all get heart attacks."

Jerry Lee and Myra Gale Lewis during happier times. "They were just jealous, just plain jealous!" was Myra Gale's plaintive cry regarding all the bad press the couple received regarding their marriage.

JOHNNY PAYCHECK, who shot a man point-blank during a drunken argument in a bar in 1985, and earned himself two years in the Chillicothe (Ohio) Correctional Institute. (Take This Jail and Shove It...?) He also nearly beat a superior officer to death while in the navy twenty-five years before that incident. Johnny's thought of the day: "I'll do whatever I damn well please."

GLEN CAMPBELL, who was charged in a $3 million lawsuit by former live-in lover Tanya Tucker with "Battery, Mayhem, and Assault with a deadly weapon." "She says I knocked her teeth out. She's lying," Campbell countered. As both of them were ingesting copious amounts of cocaine at the time (which Glen admits to in his 1994 autobiography, *Rhinestone Cowboy*), it's entirely possible that they're both telling the truth as they remember it. (The suit was settled out of court, but the terms were never disclosed; it's even possible that no money changed hands.) But his finding God doesn't seem to have tempered Campbell's memories of their time together, which include such precious moments as Tanya walking through a plate-glass window while stoned and Glen nearly killing himself while freebasing.

Bibliography

Campbell, Glen. *Rhinestone Cowboy*. New York: Villard, 1994.

Carr, Patrick, ed. *The Illustrated History of Country Music*. New York: Dolphin Books, 1980.

Hume, Martha. *You're So Cold I'm Turning Blue*. New York: Viking, 1982.

Millard, Bob. *Country Music: Seventy Years of America's Favorite Music*. New York: HarperPerennial, 1993.

Reise, Randall. *Nashville Babylon*. New York: Congdon & Weed, 1988.

Richards, Tad, and Melvin B. Shestack. *The New Country Music Encyclopedia*. New York: Fireside, 1993.

Roland, Tom. *The Billboard Book of Number One Country Hits*. New York: Billboard Books, 1991.

Rovin, Jeff. *Country Music Babylon*. New York: St. Martin's, 1993.

Tosches, Nick. *Hellfire: The Jerry Lee Lewis Story*. New York: Dell, 1982.

The author also wishes to acknowledge such indispensable publications as *Country Music*, *Entertainment Weekly*, and *People*, several years' worth of which were consulted along the way.

Photography Credits

Index